BUNDLE BOOK

Positive Puppy Training 101 .... *2*

Positive Dog Training 101 .... *91*

Positive Puppy Training 101

The Ultimate Practical Guide to Raising an Amazing and Happy Dog Without Causing Your Dog Stress or Harm With Modern Training Methods

Table of Contents

Introduction 6

Going Positive 7

    THE BENEFITS 8

    THE REWARDS 10

Home Sweet Home 13

    SHOPPING FOR THE ESSENTIALS 13

    PUPPY-PROOFING YOUR HOUSE 17

    GETTING INTRODUCED 19

The Food Dilemma 23

House Training Your Puppy 26

    GETTING USED TO THE CRATE 26

    LEARNING TO ACCEPT THE LEASH 31

    POTTY TRAINING 36

Training Through Puppy's Growth Stages 43

    8 TO 12 WEEKS 43

    12 TO 16 WEEKS 48

    16 TO 24 WEEKS 61

    6 TO 9 MONTHS 71

    9 TO 12 MONTHS 75

Giving the Clicker a Try 77

Correcting Behavior Problems 80

    SHUSHING THE BARKER 80

    NOT ACCEPTING BITING 82

    GETTING CHEWING UNDER CONTROL 83

    STOPPING THE DIGGING FRENZY 84

    DISCOURAGING THE JUMPER 86

Dealing with Separation Anxiety 88

Conclusion 90

Introduction 94

Training with Love 95
    THE POWER OF REINFORCEMENT 95
    THE SCIENCE BEHIND POSITIVE REINFORCEMENT 100

Reinforcing Proper Behavior 102

House training an Older Dog 104
    GETTING READY 104
    CRATE TRAINING (IN 1 WEEKEND) 105
    GOING POTTY 109
    PAPER TRAINING 111

Teaching Behavior in 4 Weeks 114
    WHERE TO TRAIN BUDDY? 114
    THE BASIC FORMULA 115
    WEEK 1 TRAINING 116
    WEEK 2 TRAINING 124
    WEEK 3 TRAINING 131
    WEEK 4 TRAINING 140

Dealing with Misbehavior 148
    EXCESSIVE BARKING 148
    DISCOURAGING JUMPING UP 150
    NO BEGGING, PLEASE 153
    STOP LICKING ME... OR YOURSELF 154
    STOPPING SUBMISSIVE WETTING 156

Fun Games for Practice and Bonding 159
    HIGH-FIVE 159
    ROLL OVER 161
    TUG 162
    PLAY DEAD 163
    BELLY CRAWL 164

Take a Bow 165
Phasing Out the Treats 167
  The Food Lures 167
  The Food Rewards 168
Addressing Anxiety Correctly 170
Bonus Chapter: Agility Training 174
Conclusion 177

Introduction

Whether you are thinking about adopting a puppy or you have already added a cuddly member to your family, only to witness the exciting and cheerful moment being overshadowed by the chaos of disobedience, you are definitely in the right place. This book offers you all of the necessary tools required for instilling order from the minute you bring your bundle of joy home throughout its first year.

It doesn't matter which type of breed you own – all puppies can be trained. There is no such thing as a disobedient puppy, only an uncommitted owner. The purpose of this book is to show you, the dog owner, how to be the best trainer you can be, and help your puppy grow into a healthy, obedient, and happy dog.

The training success depends on how effective your communication is and just how committed you are to do the training drills on a daily basis. But, training your puppy shouldn't be a task you can hardly get through. It should be a fun and enjoyable time for both of you that will result in a strong and positive dog-owner relationship.

Revealing to you the secrets of positive reinforcement and teaching you how to approach your training process with the puppy's growth stages in mind, this book contains everything you need in order to instill proper discipline during the first and trickiest year of your dog's life. From how to prepare your house for your puppy, teach him that his teeth are not for your new shoes, to training him to become a respectful and obedient dog, this guide will show you that training your puppy is something that you will look forward to.

Now, grab some doggy treats and jump to the first chapter to learn all about training with love.

Going Positive

If the cuddly addition to your family is not your first interaction with dogs, then you are probably well aware that getting your dog to resist the urge to chew on your new sofa is not an easy task. It requires time, love, commitment, and most importantly patience. But luckily for the dog owners, puppies are just like babies. They are incredibly adaptive creatures that can soak your commands in like sponges. But the way in which you tell your puppy to sit or stop barking is of crucial importance, not only for the success of the training process but for the strength of your relationship with the dog, as well.

If you are thinking about taking the heavy-handed approach just because that's how dogs were trained in your time, you are making a huge mistake. In order for you to form a loving relationship with your puppy and help him grow into an obedient dog, you need to step away from the traditional methods.

Traditional training methods involve a leash that is used to correct the dog's behavior, such as pulling on the training leash when walking. But besides being cruel, traditional puppy training is also inefficient in most cases because the dog ends up feeling the strength of the leash often too late, and the training process becomes a painful and confusing process for the puppy. Not to mention that you cannot traditionally train a young puppy as all that pulling can end up causing neck injuries.

Choosing to go positive, on the other hand, is the best way to ensure that your puppy will be trained the right way while feeling loved at the same time. **Positive reinforcement** uses non-confrontational training methods in order to work your puppy's brain – by giving them rewards for positive behavior.

This training method has become extremely popular in the last decade as it has been promoted by some of the best dog trainers (such as Dawn Sylvia-Stasiewicz who used this method to train Bo, the Obama's dog).

The concept behind positive reinforcement training is pretty simple – by rewarding the good behavior you increase the chances of it being repeated. And the best part? This training method can be started the day you bring your pup home – any puppy can handle getting treats and being praised. Just keep in mind that the only way this training can work is if you reward the desired behavior immediately after it happens. That way your puppy can associate the reward with that behavior and become encouraged to repeat it again in the future. Obviously, the more you praise, the better your pup will learn what behavior gives him the treats and what doesn't.

The Benefits

Positive reinforcement is the only training method that is suitable for young puppies and therefore, very appealing to dog owners. It allows you to establish ground rules and proper behavior in a pretty short amount of time. And time is usually what dog owners are concerned with the most when deciding on how to train their puppies, once you begin this journey, you will soon realize that being a fast and effective training method is actually not the best thing about positive reinforcement. It is actually the fact that it's a fun process that boosts the confidence and enthusiasm in your puppy and you as its owner.

Besides being the most humane way to teach obedience, choosing to train your puppy with praising and rewards will throw many other benefits your way:

Training for Everyone

Unlike other training methods that put only one person in charge in order to show dominance that the puppy should obey, positive reinforcement allows everyone in the family to become a part of the training process. This method can never result in danger. For instance, unlike the traditional training where a child pulling on a leash or using another correction method can hurt the puppy (or in some cases even the child), teaching your child the commands you are using and filling their pockets with doggy treats can be nothing but fun.

Communication Establishment

Positive reinforcement is the only way in which you can establish solid communication with your puppy. You use a command to tell your puppy what to do, and then give rewards when the desired action is completed. When you start praising after every good behavior, your dog will be motivated and encouraged to repeat those actions as it is in their nature to please. This will allow you to communicate with the puppy in a clear way.

Punishing in order to correct behavior and teach a new one is not always so clear. Imagine your puppy has urinated on your new carpet. You use the old trick by smacking it with a rolled-up newspaper with the purpose of teaching that urinating on carpets is off limits. But, the chances of your puppy misinterpreting your intention are pretty high. For instance, your puppy could associate the punishment with not being allowed to urinate in your presence, which is why many dog owners who use traditional training never seem to catch their puppies and older dogs in the act of making a mess. Instead, the dogs have accidents when alone. That is clearly a problem in communication as fear is not an effective way to instill order.

Using rewards to praise, on the other hand, will result in no confusion. Your puppy will clearly detect why it is being rewarded, which will encourage it to repeat the desired behavior.

Perfect for All Breeds

Besides being cruel, traditional training methods like leash correction and other forms of punishments are not that effective, simply because they are not suitable for every breed type. Some dog types that are aggressive in nature can become even more aggressive when faced with punishments. On the other hand, fearful dogs can become even more fearful and may not respond well to even the smallest form of behavioral correction.

Trainers who use positive reinforcement have reported effectiveness and success in training all breeds, aggressive and fearful dogs included. This training method can be used for a variety of behaviors, so no matter what type of puppy you are thinking about adopting, positive reinforcement can definitely help you establish good communication and teach proper habits.

Bond Strengthening

If you are thinking about getting a puppy or have already adopted one, then chances are, you want it to become a part of your family and to be your companion and friend. Choosing to teach obedience with positive reinforcement is the perfect way to strengthen the dog-owner relationship. The difference between this training method and the outdated, traditional ones, is that positive reinforcement helps you not only to teach your puppy how to behave, but it also allows you to establish trust and strengthen the bond between the two of you.

Try to look at things from the puppy's perspective. Would you be more comfortable to work in a firm where the boss rewards you for finishing important projects or where you are physically forced and pushed to get things done? Your puppy is more likely to enjoy spending time with you if your communication is positive and if you praise the proper behavior.

Mental Stimulation

The most common behavioral problems arise out of boredom. If your puppy's day is not fulfilled and is left to sit around the house or backyard all day, it will try to tell you that in the form of digging, scratching, or chewing. By having a couple of positive training sessions each day, your puppy will burn enough energy to keep it content and not get bored.

It's Fun!

If your training is positive, upbeat, and short, it may turn out to be a lot of fun, not only for your puppy but for you too. By praising and rewarding, your puppy will quickly realize that good behavior leads to its favorite treats and therefore will try to repeat those actions in the hopes of being rewarded. Shortly after starting the positive reinforcement training, your puppy will look at the sessions as playtime, so teaching him new commands will be a breeze for you both.

The Rewards

The core of positive reinforcement is the reward. In order to reinforce a behavior that you like, you give your puppy a reward for the performed action to encourage it to associate the action with the reward, learn the behavioral pattern that gives it the treat and repeat it again in the future.

Those who choose other training methods usually step away from positive reinforcement because they look at the rewards as bribes. Like luring a three-year-old with chocolate to get them to listen to you, day after day. But bribing and rewarding are very different things. Think of your paycheck for a second. Does your boss bribe you with money to get you to work and contribute to the firm? No – you are rewarded for your hard work at the end of each month. If you stop getting paid for your work, you will not only decrease your performance but will actually stop coming to work. The same thing goes for your puppy. If it doesn't have a stimulus that will encourage it to behave in a certain way, it will not bother to complete the desired action. It's as simple as that.

But, even though the first thing that comes to mind when thinking about rewarding a puppy is small bone-shaped doggy treats, there are many different ways in which you can reward your dog's good behavior. Each dog is different and not all puppies respond the same to things. Knowing what your puppy is like and finding out what motivates it can help you train your pooch with success and have tons of fun along the way.

Treats

Treats are the most common reward for a reason. They are easy to dispense and perfect for giving an immediate reward. Besides, food is what most pups are interested in the most, so that's a pretty good reason to fill your pockets with tiny doggy treats when heading to the park. When trying to successfully train a puppy in a short amount of time, rewarding them with doggy treats is the best choice.

So, why someone would choose another reward, you may wonder. Besides the fact that some people find carrying treats around to be inconvenient, many pups who have digestive issues, weight problems, or are struggling with food allergies, should be rewarded another way.

Games

Just like treats, puppies love playing games. Spend some time with your pup trying out different games and see what it enjoys the most. Give your pooch a command in order for it to perform an action, and as soon as it does it, initiate its favorite game. That could be anything that the two of you have fun doing, or you can play it safe with a game of fetch, tug-of-war, or another classic.

Attention

All dogs love getting attention, but some more than others. If you see that your dog wants nothing more than being lavished with attention, you can actually use this as a reward for teaching it proper behavior. Wait for your dog to come to you for petting, but instead of immediately showering it with love, make it work for your attention. Give it a simple command like sitting down, and wait for it to do it. When your puppy finally does what it was told to, set aside some time for snuggling. If it doesn't do what was asked of it, step aside for 15-20 seconds, then return and try again. Shortly after trying this trick, your puppy will understand that completing the desired action means it is rewarded with hugs and smooches, so will be encouraged to behave properly and learn new commands.

Going Outdoors

Of course, this cannot actually be used for every *Sit* or *Stay* command, but at times, allowing your puppy access to the outdoors can also be used as a great reward to reinforce positive behavior. For instance, this can be quite beneficial when house training your pup. Put on the leash and take your puppy outdoors, to the spot where you like it to eliminate its waste. Do not let him sniff around and explore, but just wait for him to relieve himself. If your pup doesn't urinate, go back inside and try again later. When it finally relieves itself, praise it, and take it for a walk, allowing it to stop and explore as much as it likes. If your dog loves the outdoors, it will soon associate the spot for eliminating waste as access to the interesting sights and new smells, which will encourage it to relieve itself each time you bring it to that designated spot.

Giving your puppy treats seems to always do the trick, and this book will use that reward for the training sessions explained within. If you, for some reason, decide on another reward, the most important thing you need to have in mind is to reward your puppy immediately after it completes the desired action. Otherwise, the training will become an ineffective, long, and confusing process for both of you.

Home Sweet Home

Congratulations! You are about to add a new member to your family. But as eager as you may be to bring your buddy home, there are some things you need to tackle first in order to make sure that your home is not only appropriate for such a young pup, but also to help your pooch adapt to the new, strange environment. From what you should buy for your bundle of joy, how to organize your home so that it's safe for your puppy, to getting advice on making the first introductions, this chapter will help you get ready for your puppy's long-awaited arrival.

Shopping for the Essentials

My bet is, you have already spent some time online researching your puppy's breed to prepare for its arrival. But despite the fact that you have spent hours trying to write down a list of things that it will love, you have probably stumbled upon conflicting theories and different opinions. For some pups, such and such a toy was best, while others became aggressive at its sight. Some puppies preferred sleeping on a certain type of bedding, while others wanted to sleep on the floor tiles. You've read stories of how purchasing the most expensive crate will help you potty train your pup, but many also had a house training success with nothing but a gated corner in the kitchen.

Visiting a pet store doesn't help you clear your confusion either. With more choices than a toy store, shopping for your puppy's arrival can easily turn from exciting into daunting. So, what is the right choice? If you want to spare your budget (as well as your mind) from being blown, you should only stick to the essentials. Though you may be tempted to buy all sorts of different gadgets, leave that for later. Make sure that you have just the things your pup absolutely needs for the first couple of weeks. After you get to know your pup and discover its nature, the trip to the pet store will not be such a mind-boggling experience anymore, and you will know exactly what to buy.

Food and Treats

There are a lot of different types of doggy foods and treats. Although your puppy will probably be happy with pretty much anything that is made for puppies, you need to choose the right type depending on its breed and unique condition. Talk to its veterinarian and ask for advice. If your puppy has a special medical condition or food allergies, it goes without saying that you will have to be extra careful when purchasing its food and treats.

Bowls

Your puppy needs two bowls: one for doggy food and one for water. What you need to have in mind when purchasing bowls for your puppy, is their size and the material that they're made of.

Buy smaller bowls where your pup can easily reach its food and water. The best material choice is by far stainless steel, as it cannot break, it is heavy enough not to get knocked over every time it wants a sip, and it is the most durable. Ceramic bowls are not recommended because they can easily break. If plastic is your preferred choice, keep in mind that your pup will most likely chew on its bowl and make a mess, and there's also the chance of it developing a reaction that can cause nose discoloration.

Collar

Though you may want to reach for the one that you think looks best, when it comes to choosing a collar, the color and printed design is the least important factor you should look for. If planning on house training your pup, it is recommended for you to buy not one, but two collars:

<u>Training Collar</u> - Purchasing a special collar for the training practice is highly recommended. That way you can make sure that your puppy is easy to guide when on a leash, which will be much appreciated until your pup learns proper leash walking.

There are two types of training collars that you can choose from:

1. No-Pull Harness – This is a collar that goes around the puppy's chest instead of its neck. It is specially designed to discourage puppies from pulling on a leash. For safety reasons, this is the recommended option as it prevents from choking.

2. Martingale Collar – This collar is also called the *limited-slip* collar, as it prevents your pup to back out of it when it starts pulling. And if your dog has a longer neck, such as a Greyhound, for instance, this is by far the best collar option.

<u>Buckle Collar</u> – When you're not training your pup, it's better to leave a buckle collar on. The buckle collar should also have an ID tag attached, in case of emergencies. It is not

recommended to be training your pup with a buckle collar on as you will not have the same amount of control as with a training collar. Besides, if your pup grows to be much stronger than anticipated, the training can become pretty inconvenient.

Leash

Whether leather, cotton web, or nylon, no matter what material the leash is made of, the important thing to look for when buying a leash is only the length. The perfect lash is 6-foot long, however, if you want to let your pup run around your backyard without you guiding your way, you can consider buying a long line (30-foot long).

Purchase the leash with the training process in mind. It is not about the strength, but about teaching with finesse. The leash should be light and easy for you to handle. Stay away from heavy and inconvenient chain leashes.

Crate

Do not let the cage-like look of the crate discourage you from buying one. Your pup needs a cozy, den-like space that is clean, enclosed, and most importantly, only theirs. The crate will be its place to rest and it will also help it feel safe while you are away. Think of the crate, not like a cage but more like a baby crib. You wouldn't leave your baby to sleep in the middle of a large, open, and unprotected room, right?

And just like with a baby's crib, buying a crate for your puppy is also not that simple. You will have many different options that come in different sizes, colors, and materials. Not to get too overwhelming, here are some tips that can help you find the perfect one for your pup:

- Before buying a crate, do some research and find out exactly how much your puppy will grow, in order to make the right choice.

- Keep in mind that your pup grows very quickly, so buying the smallest one may not be a perfect choice, unless you want to keep spending your money, that is. For best results, buy a size-adjustable crate that you can use while your puppy is still young, but also when he reaches adulthood.

- If you cannot find a size-adjustable crate, do not despair. Just shrink the space with the use of some pillows, since sleeping in a large crate will encourage your pooch to eliminate waste inside.

- If you plan on traveling a lot, buy a plastic crate for your convenience.
- If you're not traveling, stick to a wire crate. Despite their cage-like look, they do offer the best airflow and visibility and are therefore recommended.

Gate

Gates can be super beneficial if you have a staircase in your home that you want to block, keep your pup away from dangerous areas or an off-limits room, or simply if you want to close off a room to play with your pooch or even supervise.

Do not think that closing off space and gating larger areas is cruel. Quite the contrary. Puppies feel lonely and forgotten in large spaces, so providing an enclosed area for your pooch to play is recommended.

Toys

Puppies love bouncy and squeaky things. They don't care if it is red, green, or if it costs $1 or $15. But, despite the fact that your pooch will be satisfied with anything it can chew on, it is your job to offer only the quality toys.

And quality doesn't often mean expensive. When buying toys for your puppy, the most important thing for you to have in mind is for the toys to be appropriate and safe to chew on:

- Squeaky toys will keep boredom at bay and are great if you to want to be involved in the game
- Chew toys are perfect for mental stimulation and healthy gums. Just make sure they are appropriate for your pup
- You can also buy a rope, ball, or a Frisbee, for an interactive game
- Never let your pup play with tennis balls or sticks. These are not dog-appropriate toys and chewing on these can cause damage. Ask for advice on what toys are best for the size and breed of your pup.

Shampoo and Brush

Hygiene always comes first. And while you wouldn't have to bathe your puppy the first weeks of its life, having shampoo and a brush for him in your home, is essential. Tell the pet store salesperson what breed you are looking to buy a shampoo and a brush for and ask for some advice.

Puppy-Proofing Your House

Just like with toddlers, your house also has to be puppy-proofed, not only so that your puppy will not destroy your belongings, but most importantly so that you can prevent any injuries.

The average home is a real hazard for puppies, in most cases. Dogs are extremely curious animals by nature, and in order to prevent your puppy from chewing on something from under the sink or choking on a piece of wire, you need to secure your entire house before your pup gets home.

Here are some tips on how you transform your cluttered house into a puppy-safe environment:

Locked Cabinets and High Shelves. The very first thing you need to do is take all of the hazardous items, and place them somewhere where your pup cannot reach. The high shelves are perfect for this, and you can also lock up your cabinets to make sure that your puppy cannot get there. If the cabinets can be locked, perfect. If not, consider purchasing some childproof latches to increase security.

The items that you have to keep away from your pup include:

- Medication
- Plastic Bags
- Food Waste
- Cleaning Products and other Chemicals
- Cosmetic Products and Make-Up
- Children's Toys
- Valuable Items that You Don't Want to be Destroyed

Keep the Cabinets Closed. Besides locking up the cabinets, you need to adopt a habit of actually keeping them closed and locked. Rummaging through open cabinets is like searching for a mysterious treasure for puppies. To prevent your puppy from swallowing or choking on something, you need to keep everything closed. Appliances such as a dishwasher or washing machine should also be kept closed.

Keep Food Out of Reach. Most food items are also hazardous for your puppy. Food such as chocolate, onions, or coffee, can make your pooch really sick. Make sure to store your food properly and do not leave half-eaten things lying around your kitchen. The same thing goes for glasses.

Here are some tips on how to keep food away from your puppy:

- Store your fruits and veggies in hanging baskets.

- Secure your foods inside your pantry, fridge, and cabinets.

- Dog's food also has to be secured in a food container.

- Make sure to throw away wrappers and peels and keep them out of reach.

- Packaged foods should also be kept off of counters.

Keep Houseplants Away. You may not be aware, but most of the common houseplants actually present a hazard to your puppy. It is recommended that you check if your houseplants are toxic or not, and ultimately, keep all of your plants in hanging baskets or on a high shelf.

Organize the Wires. In most households, there can be found wires hanging out on every appliance. Many pups are actually drawn to these wires, and it really goes without saying how dangerous they can be for them. Make sure to organize the cords in your room and keep the wires tucked behind pieces of furniture. You can also secure your wires by gathering them up in a slack and then tying with a zip tie. Keep your chargers and portable electronic devices out of reach, as well.

Secure the Fireplace. The fireplace can also be a safety hazard. When your pup gets all excited chasing a ball or playing a fun game, it can easily fall into the fireplace. And since dogs can also experience tunnel vision when they are all wired up, you can see how dangerous this can be.

Installing a fireplace screen or a gate can be of great help. Fireplace gates can be found not only in the furniture stores, but in most well-equipped pet stores, as well.

Secure the Backyard. If you have a backyard, chances are, your pooch will be spending most of its time there. But, besides offering freedom, your yard can also pose a danger to your puppy.

Here are some tips on how to make it a secure and safe place for your puppy:

- Secure the gate. If you are planning on letting your puppy spend unsupervised time in the yard, the first thing you need to make sure is that your gate and fence are secure. Keep in mind that dogs are great diggers, so place some large rocks near the fence's base if necessary, so your pup cannot slip under.

- Do not use pesticides. If gardening is your hobby, make sure to keep your garden alive without pesticides, as most of them can make your pup really ill. When buying lawn and garden products, make sure to look for the "pet safe" sign written on the label.

- Keep the tools out of reach. Tools, as well as, smaller objects such as screws and nails, sharp things, and car parts, should be put on a shelf in the garage, or stored in a place that your puppy will not have access to.

- Clean anti-freeze. Anti-freeze is a real threat to dogs because it is extremely toxic, and dogs are attracted to its specific smell. If you believe that there might be some anti-freeze on the driveway or your garage floor, you will have to thoroughly clean that area, to prevent the puppy from licking it.

- Auto chemicals, rat poison, mothballs, and other poisonous things, should always be locked away and kept out of reach.

Getting Introduced

When it comes to bringing your pup home, the most important thing that you need to have in mind for that first day, is to let it be your puppy's day. Your pup is not just something you've brought home from the store. It is a living creature that feels things just as deeply as us humans. Try to keep your home absolutely stress-free for the first 24 hours at least, and reschedule all of your appointments.

-If you have kids, make sure to keep them calm (use tasty bribes if necessary). The point is to welcome your puppy the right way, not to get it all riled up so it starts nipping and jumping around like crazy.

A Welcome Circle

They say that first impressions are usually right. Make sure to give your puppy the best first impression. The important thing is for him to feel welcome and safe in its new home. For that purpose, you can create a welcome circle:

1. Have all of the family members sit on the floor, in a circle.

2. Give everyone a couple of doggy treats.

3. Create a circle with your legs, by spreading them out so your feet will touch.

4. Place your puppy in the middle.

5. Let everyone give the puppy a treat and pet it. If you have kids, make sure to teach him how to pet and hold your puppy properly, before it arrives home.

What About Other Pets?

Resident pets are, in most cases, not thrilled about sharing their living space with another animal. Small puppies tend to be annoying to other pets, and the attention oodles that your puppy may be getting can affect your other pet in a negative way. It might take some time for them to get to know each other, so be prepared.

It may take a while for your pets to get used to one another, but there are some things you can do to knock down the tension a bit:

Introduce with Smell, First. Before you introduce the pets with each other, make sure to get them used to their smell, first. Animals are smell sensitive, and by getting them introduced with the smell of the other pet first, you lower the surprise effect when they actually get to meet.

Put the Resident Pets First. The puppy's reaction is important, but what's important is for it to feel welcome. For that purpose, you may need to keep jealousy at bay so that your older pets don't start taking their dissatisfaction out on the puppy.

There are several ways to do this:

- Feed them first

- When entering the door, greet them first

- If your older pet is also a dog, let it pass first (whether through doorways or when climbing stairs)

- If your older pet approaches you while you're interacting with the pup, turn away from it for a minute and address the other pet instantly

- Treat and play with them first

Don't be afraid that your new pup will be said if it looks like you're giving most of the attention to the other pet. That way you will teach your puppy to grow into respecting the resident pet and to act accordingly.

Keep the Puppy in a Confined Area. If you think that there will be a lot of tension between the two pets, knowing the behavior of your resident pet, you should plan ahead about keeping the puppy in a confined area. If you, however, decide on a place where the older pet used to eat, make sure to change the feeding area, at least 7-10 days before your puppy arrives home.

For Cats, Let Them Introduce Themselves. If your resident pet is a cat, do not try to use force, but let it introduce itself in its own time. Whether it will be fearful or not, try to give it access to the area where your pup is, but, do not try to push it to enter the room. When your cat is ready to get closer to the puppy, let the cat wander around the room, but only at its own will. If your pup turns wild and starts acting like crazy, enter the room and try to calm it down.

Surviving the First Week

You've finally made it home! You may want to speed things up a bit and take your pup on a full tour of the house or put it on a leash and take it to the dog park, but don't let over excitement clout your judgment. Your pup is still young, and in its eyes, everything is brand new and confusing. Give it some time to adjust first. Take this slow the first week, so you can both adapt – your puppy to its new house, and you to your new family member.

The First Day

Although it is the most exciting, keep your expectations about the first day as low as possible. After all the anticipation, your pup is finally home, however, your introduction may not be what you've envisioned. Most dog owners have said that the first day is typically odd, so don't expect too much from your pup then.

On the very first day, pretty much anything can happen. Your pup may be overly excited and jumpy, it might just step right into the mix, or it may even be sleepy and a bit isolated. Whatever its reaction is, know that it is perfectly normal. After all, this is a brand new adventure for your puppy, and it may not feel prepared just yet. Give it time to adjust.

Enclose the puppy in a room the first day and supervise it at all times. Spend some time observing it and its reaction, and make sure to reflect its interests in a calm and positive way. The most important thing is not to overwhelm it right from the start, so it can get used to things easily.

Days 2-7

Unlike the first day, the rest of the first week will be pretty progressive. Even by day 2, you will notice changes in your pup's behavior, and it will most likely start accepting the situation (and the people) around it better.

Make sure to spend some time bonding and getting to know each other. Leave the training session for later, and just be with your pup. If it is chewing things, try to simply use a taste deterrent the first week. Again, do not overwhelm it. Be positive and talk to your puppy in a cheerful way.

The Food Dilemma

What should you give your pup to eat? How much should your puppy eat? What to use as a treat? These are all questions that new dog owners are most likely to ask themselves when thinking about adopting a puppy and training it to become an obedient adult dog.

Walking down the food dog aisle only makes things more complicated. Unlike back in the day when there were one or two types of dog food, today, the choices are pretty endless. But, that's a good thing. Specialized dieting formulas and high-quality foods with essential sourcing contribute to the overall health of your puppy.

But, despite the obvious reason why you should choose quality ingredients for your pup – which is providing your puppy with a balanced diet rich in essential nutrients, something else can benefit from balanced meals besides your puppy's health, and that is its training success.

Many dog owners overlook the importance that the food has over the process of training, but the truth is, even the simplest directions can take a lot of time to teach if your pup is under or overfed.

Your pup will be the happiest if it has a predictable feeding routine, so make sure to provide that. Besides the fact that it thrives when a consistent schedule has been set, the regular feeding times can also support the house training process. Knowing exactly when and how much your pup has eaten makes it a lot easier for you to determine its potty needs, which can be a lifesaver when training your puppy to accept his drop zone.

The Feeding Schedule

But just how much should your pup eat? Most new dog owners make the mistake of overfeeding their puppies, who then refuse to cooperate during the training session, and the whole process is one overwhelming experience. To avoid that, you need to set a consistent routine from the start. Here is a timeline for your puppy's first year. Stick to it.

6 to 10 Weeks – 4 feedings a day

10 Weeks to 4 Months – Decrease the feedings to 3 times a day

4 to 6 Months – 2 feedings a day

6 to 12 Months – After your pup has reached his 6th month, you can drop his feeding to one time a day

What to Feed and How Much?

There is a difference between dog and puppy food. Puppy food is specially formulated to meet the needs of young puppies and help them develop normally while providing all of the essential nutrients. Switching to adult dog food will only rob your pooch from these nutrients. Make sure to stick to puppy food throughout the first year.

And if you are wondering whether paying the big bucks really makes the difference, of course. If you can afford premium food for your puppy, know that you will be getting high quality and nutritional diversity in return. If you cannot, however, don't worry. Ask your veterinarian to give you advice on how to provide the best nutritional value for your pup.

As for how much to feed your pup, that really depends. Small breeds need, obviously, smaller portions than large puppies. But there isn't a set rule, really. The only thing you can do is to watch your pup closely, not his bowl. Through a trial and error, you will be able to determine the exact amount of food your puppy needs. If your puppy skips a meal here and there, or it picks at its food, that is usually a sign that you are either supposed to eliminate one feeding, or that you are simply giving him more food than necessary.

The Treats

The treats are the most important factor in the process of positive training. Without these tasty rewards, your pup will not be encouraged to participate in the sessions and go through all the trouble of getting your directions right.

But, what exactly is a treat? Should you pay tons of money for the most expensive smelly bones just for the sake of luring your pooch to show a shred of interest in the training? Of course, not. The treat can be pretty much anything your puppy loves to eat, even regular dog food. In fact, most dog trainers suggest that the treat should be a mixture of regular food and more special pieces of treats.

The most important thing is for the treats to be:

- Chewy

- Rich in Aroma and Flavor

- Easy to Break

- Soft

Start with a small number of treats and mix them up with doggy food. As the training progresses, increase the treats gradually. Also, make sure to use different treats on a weekly basis, so that your pup doesn't lose interest for cooperating. Treats can be pretty much anything your puppy enjoys – from special bone-shaped doggy treats, to small pieces of cheese or sausage.

House Training Your Puppy

House training is one of the very first things that you need to teach your puppy. It should be started the minute you bring your pooch home, but don't expect to reap the benefits too soon. House training a pup can be a long process, so if you aren't armed with the right amount of patience, you are in for some disappointment.

Puppies are stubborn, naughty, and they just love to push your boundaries. You need to be seriously committed if you want to succeed, and most importantly, to develop a consistent routine that will help your pooch learn.

The general rule of thumb is that puppies can be successfully house trained by the time they are 14-16 weeks old. If you have brought your puppy home with just 8 weeks, you can expect earlier results, sure. Just don't keep your hopes too high and remember that puppies don't really start learning until they reach their 12th week.

Regardless of your pup's current age, the guidelines of this chapter can help you have a housetrained pup in just a few weeks. As long as you obey the four house training rules, you will manage to create a healthy learning environment for your puppy:

1. Praise your pup immediately after it behaves
2. Keep a solid and consistent routine
3. Never punish your pup physically if it has an accident
4. Do not correct your puppy unless you catch it in the act

Getting Used to the Crate

The idea of being locked up is no more appealing to dogs than it is to humans. No one wants to have its freedom limited, so don't think that just because you've purchased an expensive crate your pup will fall in love with it the minute it steps inside. Chances are, you will have to train your pup to become used to its crate and love spending time there.

Many novices think of crate training as confining and not that natural, but the truth is, dogs are den animals by nature. They may not be thrilled about being locked up, that's for sure, but their instinct tells them that they should have a safe place of their own. Providing a crate is not cruel but comforting.

But, just because your pup doesn't perceive the crate as its safe spot just yet doesn't mean that you cannot change its point of view and make it realize that the crate is the perfect resting place for it. And since puppies have absolutely no preconceived notions, incorporating a few tricks in order to train your puppy to love its crate is indeed possible.

Assuming that you've already purchased the appropriate crate for your pup and that you got the size right, you can now follow these next steps to create your puppy's safe haven and get it to love it:

Step #1: Find the Perfect Spot

Many dog owners tend to overlook this one, which is exactly why they experience resistance and cannot crate train their puppies properly. You may think that the place where you'll put the crate doesn't really matter as long as it is dry and clean, but it can have a huge impact on how your pup is going to respond to its new home.

Imagine your family locks you up in the basement and they go upstairs to spend a lazy afternoon in the family room. How would you feel? No one wants to be isolated. Dogs are social animals by nature and they love to feel like they belong to the pack. Here, the pack is your family. So set some room aside and make sure that you put the crate someplace where you and your family spend most of your time during the day, such as the living room or the kitchen. Otherwise, the crate will only feel like an isolating punishment and you will never be able to train your pup to love it.

Step #2: Make It Comfortable

In order for your pooch to feel secure in its crate, it has to provide comfort. You can easily create an atmosphere that is more den-like for your puppy, by putting a blanket (or a towel) on the bottom, so that your pup can sleep comfortably in it. If you have bought a wire or a mesh crate, you can also find a breathable blanket to place over the top, so your puppy can have a space that is only theirs and where it can rest peacefully.

Keep in mind that if your pooch is very prone to chewing on things, it may find the bedding to be a perfect toy. If that is the case with your puppy, remove everything from the crate and do not add anything on the bottom of the crate. Wait until your pup matures a bit before you make a bed inside the crate for it.

Step #3: Show Enthusiasm

The more enthusiasm you show for the crate, the more excited your pooch will be. As you set up its safe haven, chances are, your puppy will come over to give it a sniff and explore it. Once it is close to the crate, get all excited and start saying positive things about the crate. It may seem silly to you, however, trying to trick puppies into giving their crate a try with a happy tone almost always does the trick. Just speak positively and wait to see if your puppy will get inside on its own. Do not force it to step into the crate as that will only help your puppy get more scared of it.

Step #4: Open the Door

Once the crate is all set up and your pup has had the time to explore it (even if only from the outside), it is time to start training your puppy to fall in love with it. Keep in mind that this is a slow and gradual process, so do not try to rush things.

Start by opening the door of the crate. The second the door is opened, start encouraging your puppy to go inside by saying positive things. It may not be so easily convinced to check it out at this moment, but know that that's perfectly normal. The crate is still perceived as a big, strange object in your living room, so give it some time to get used to it.

If you convince your pup to go inside, however, be sure to immediately praise and reward your puppy for it, and by all means, do not close the door of the crate when it enters it. That will only create a feeling of entrapment and get your pup all scared. You need to make sure that your puppy is comfortable and feels secure when inside before you can think about closing it in.

Step #5: Leave Treats and Toys Inside

If your pup doesn't show enthusiasm and isn't particularly interested in seeing what's inside the crate, try to encourage it to check it out by leaving some of its favorite doggy treats inside the crate. Start by placing the treats where your pup can reach them even without getting inside. It is perfectly normal for your pooch to just poke his head inside and get the treats – let him. Praise your puppy after doing so and keep placing treats inside, but leave them further and further inside the crate, each time, to try to lure your puppy inside. Just don't forget the most important part – praise and reward.

If your puppy is not responding well to treats, try the same trick with its favorite toy, or with a brand new one that it hasn't gotten the chance to explore and chew on just yet.

Step #6: Feed Him Inside

The point of crate training is to help your puppy get comfortable with spending time inside the crate. And to do that, it will have to actually spend some time inside. If it enters voluntarily to get its treats or toy from inside the crate, you have already made great progress. However, unless your puppy decides to lay down inside and play with its toy there, you will have to trick it into staying more than a second inside the crate. And the perfect way to do it is with food, of course.

Lure your puppy in with a treat or his toy, around meal time. Once it enters the crate, bring it its food bowl inside, and let it eat there. Keep the door open at all times, for the first couple of meals.

Step #7: Try Closing the Door

When your pup becomes comfortable standing and eating its meals inside the crate, it is time for you to start closing the door. Stay near the crate door so that it can see you, and while it is busy chewing its doggy food, close the door of the crate. The first couple of times, do it only for a minute or two, and gradually increase the time the door stays closed until your pup can stay inside with a closed door for 10 minutes.

Step #8: Try with Longer Stays

When your puppy has no trouble eating its meals inside the crate with the door closed, it is time to try closing it even when it's not meal time. Place a treat or a toy inside the crate and call your pup to the crate. It is recommended for you to have a command for this, such as "Kennel" or something you are comfortable with.

Encourage your puppy to get in, close the door, and then stand near the crate for the first 5-10 minutes. Then, leave the room for a minute or two. Come back to the crate and let your pooch out.

Repeat this a couple of times a day for a few days, gradually increasing the time your puppy stays inside the crate, as well as the time you spend outside the room.

Step #9: Leave the House

Once you manage to get your pup to stay inside the crate for 30 minutes straight, then it is time for you to actually crate him when you leave the house for a short outing. Of course, you need to do this only if your puppy is ready and shows no signs of distress when inside the crate.

So, take your dog out for a walk or play with it for a while to exercise it and get it tired. Put it in the crate along with its favorite toy or two and close the door. Remember, this is just the same as before. The only difference now is that you will not be in the next room, but you will actually leave your house. Make sure to leave without any fuss.

Step #10: Crate at Night

Just like you need your bed, your pup also needs its own place to sleep. The crate is not just for safety reasons. It shouldn't only be the place you put your puppy when you leave the house. It should also feel like its safe haven; a place designated for your puppy, where it can rest and sleep without being bothered. To help it understand that, you will also need to crate your puppy at night. It is strongly recommended that you put the crate in your bedroom at night, not only for practical reasons such as your puppy needing to pee during the night but also because being in the same room with you at night will help your pooch understand the whole concept of the crate better.

Step #11: Understanding How Long is Too Long

Keep in mind that your pup is a social animal who needs exercise on a regular basis. In order for it to be physically, as well as emotionally, healthy, your pooch needs regular activity. Leaving it locked up in the crate for too long can only create problems in its development.

Except at night, you should never leave your pup crated for longer than 5 hours. Here are some crate-time guidelines to help you understand just how long your puppy can be left in the crate during the early stages of its development:

<u>9-10 Weeks</u> – 30 to 60 minutes

<u>11-14 Weeks</u> – 1 to 3 hours

<u>15-16 Weeks</u> - 3-4 hours

<u>17+ Weeks</u> – 4+ hours, but <u>never</u> longer than 6 hours

Step #11: Know How to Respond to Whining

If you gave your child a chocolate bar every time it started crying, would you be raising them properly? Do not think that dogs are any different. If you do not set strict rules from the beginning, you will have serious behavior problems in the future. Pleasing the pup every time it starts whining is just like giving chocolate to a naughty three-year-old. Unless you believe your pup needs to eliminate waste, letting him out of the crate just because it is whining will have a counter effect on your crate training process. By letting your pup know that it can get more freedom if it starts whining, will only encourage this behavior and you will never be able to get your pup used to its crate.

Learning to Accept the Leash

Walking on a leash is one of the first skills that your puppy will master. Knowing leash etiquette is polite behavior that any pup should be taught from the very beginning. Proper leash manners are not only beneficial for practical purposes such as going to the groomer or having a veterinarian check, but they are also crucial for your pup's socialization and introduction to the world, in general. Knowing how to walk nicely on a leash will give your puppy more freedom to explore the outdoor wonders safely.

But, why is it important to start with leash training as soon as possible? Imagine your pup is from a larger breed. Before you know it, your small pooch will grow to be a strong and tugging tank that can pull the leash powerfully and even drag you over. This can be dangerous for various reasons. To avoid all that and provide security, your pup needs to accept the leash as early as possible.

Puppies don't know how to walk on the leash instinctively. They start pulling and get really uncomfortable once they feel the leash pressure. In order for you to avoid the leash training become a traumatic experience for your pup, you need to do it the right way.

Depending on your pup's temperament, there are three different methods in which you can introduce leash walking. Read on to choose the one that suits you and your pooch the most.

The Essentials

First of all, to get started with any of the three leash training methods, you will need 4 essential things:

1. The Collar – Your pup should have its collar around its neck in order for you to attach the leash. Make sure that the collar is comfortable around your puppy's neck and that it cannot slip out of it.

2. The Leash – For this purpose, you will need a non-retractable, regular leash.

3. The Treats – To reward and encourage leash walking, you will need tasty doggy treats. However, if your pup's a very food-motivated canine, you can use its regular food instead.

4. Patience – Keep in mind that you will need a lot of patience for this. You will need to stay calm when the puppy fights the leash and encourage proper behavior in a positive and encouraging tone. Avoid teaching leash walking when you are not in the best mood.

The Drag Method

If your pup is very young or timid, then you may find that you will need a bit more time for the drag method. That's okay! Let your pooch become accustomed to dragging its leash around before you take it a step further and decide to add pressure on the leash.

Step #1: The Collar

For you to be able to leash your pup, it has to wear its collar around its neck. Now, this probably sounds easy, but you will definitely experience resistance. Most puppies aren't comfortable with having something around their necks and they need time to adapt and get used to it. Allow it!

If you have trouble putting your puppy's collar on, follow these steps:

1. The best time to put your pup's collar on is when it is preoccupied with something else, like chewing on a rubber toy or munching on its favorite treat. Have in mind that the collar should be tightly fastened, but it should also feel comfortable. The rule of thumb says that you have fastened a comfortable collar if the collar is fastened just enough so you can slip two fingers underneath it.

2. Once the collar is on, leave it for about 10 minutes.

3. Then take it off and put it on again after 50 minutes.

4. Leave the collar on for 10 minutes at every hour, for about 2 days.

5. The third day, leave it on for 20 minutes instead of 10, again, at every hour.

6. Do this for 2 more days.

7. On the fifth day, leave the collar on at all times.

8. Leave it on for 3 days before introducing the leash.

Step #2: Attach the Leash

When your puppy is comfortable having the collar around its neck, it is time for you to attach the leash to it. Attach the leash and allow your pup to drag it around your home. Of course, shorter leashes work best for this practice, and if you have a special one without the handle to get caught on objects around your house, that would be perfect.

Step #3: Take It Outside

Go outside and allow your puppy to drag the leash there as well. Just make sure that you are keeping an eye on it. Let it drag the leash for about 4 days before taking the loose end of it. To avoid scaring your pup, do this in a calm and familiar location, such as your backyard.

Step #4: Explore

Let your pup explore while holding the loose end of the leash. Make sure not to apply pressure and let your puppy guide the way. Do this for about 10 minutes or so, and then encourage it to follow you inside, while still holding the leash loosely. If it refuses to follow you, do not drag him. Pick your puppy up and carry him inside.

Step #5: Do It Again

Over the next couple of days, take your puppy outside for at least 5-6 times. Hold the leash loosely and allow it to explore freely.

Step #6: Gentle Tugs

If you have taken your puppy outside for at least five to six times, then you are ready to apply gentle pressure to the leash. Go outside as you did before. Every three minutes or so, call your puppy in a positive tone. While doing that, gently tug the leash. If your puppy comes all encouraged and happy, praise it immediately and give it a treat. If it is not responsive and fights the leash, ignore it and wait until it stops. When it finally stops, repeat the process again. This may take longer for some puppies, but you need to have patience. The point here is for your pooch to associate the gentle tugs with positivity, so you can safely take him out for a walk.

Step #7: Practice

Practice makes perfect! Practice calling your puppy and rewarding it when it behaves, until it stops fighting the leash completely. Continue encouraging it to follow you with the leash as well as your voice, and you will have a leash trained pup in no time.

The Pressure Method

This is a bit more of an advanced, and quicker method. It doesn't include the drag routine, but it may not work if your puppy is still very young.

Step #1: The Collar and Leash

After your puppy is used to having its collar around the neck, attach its leash to it. Give it a treat after attaching the leash.

Step #2: The Tug

Once the leash is attached, pull a bit on the leash so that your pup can feel some pressure, but do not use too much force or drag your pup towards you. If your pup steps forward on its own after feeling the tug, even just a bit, praise it immediately and give it a treat.

If it begins fighting the leash, stand still and keep the leash tight. When the puppy finally stops, praise it, show it the treat, and then encourage it to come to you. When it does, give it the treat.

Step #3: Repeat

Repeat this until your pup begins coming towards you as soon as it feels the tug. Once it begins coming to you consistently, do not praise after just a few steps. Save the treat for after the pup has come all the way. Continue to praise with a positive and encouraging voice though.

Step #4: Practice

When your pup is used to come all the way to you whenever you tighten the leash gently, it is time for you to take things outside and start going out on real walks. Whenever your pup starts pulling ahead, simply stop or even change a direction so that your puppy can feel the tightening of the leash. Practice until your pup no longer pulls on the leash and follows you without any resistance.

The Wait Method

This method may take a bit longer, as you are practically doing nothing but waiting for your puppy to figure out on its own that it is supposed to come to you, but it can be extremely effective for some puppies. If the previous two methods don't quite work for you, give the 'wait' technique a try.

Step #1: The Collar and Leash

Just like before, your pup needs to be used to the collar in order to leash train it. If it is used to it, attach the leash to the collar.

Step #2: Hold and Stand Still

Take the leash with one hand and stand still. Do not move nor call your puppy. Even if it starts pulling, stand still and don't let go. The point here is to wait for the puppy to come to the end of the leash on its own. This may take a few minutes, so be patient.

Step #3: Praise and Reward

If your pup starts fighting the leash when it gets to the end of it, wait for it to stop. Once it does that, praise it immediately and reward with a treat. If it doesn't fight or pull, obviously, you praise and reward right away.

Step #4: Create a Slight Tension

Once your pup stops pulling and is no longer fighting the leash, take a step or two away from it, just enough for the leash to become slightly tighter and create a gentle pressure. If it starts fighting it now, wait for it to stop. Praise and reward when it does. Once you reward, release the tension immediately.

Step #5: Practice

Repeat it all for as long as it takes for your puppy to learn that feeling a slight tension around its neck means it should come to you, follow you, and eventually, walk nicely by your side.

Keep in mind that this is not the same as traditional training. You will not be pulling the leash for correcting your pup. You are simply teaching it to get used to sometimes feeling a slight pressure around its neck, in order to prevent unwanted behavior during one of its walks later on.

Potty Training

Although it may seem to you that puppies do nothing but chew on things all day long, believe it or not, their potty activities actually follow a pattern: eat → drink → rest (or move out of isolation) → play → chew. It is important for you to keep a close eye on your pup and take it outside after each activity in order to establish a healthy potty routine.

Even though this seems like a lot of potty runs and despite the fact that your 8-10-week old pup cannot really control its impulses, taking it to its drop zone often (even if inside the house) and letting it try to eliminate waste there will actually lay out the foundation of its understanding on how to "hold it in".

Time + Direction + Consistency

If you haven't had the opportunity to potty train a pup or a child, you are definitely in for some surprises. It takes a lot of effort, time, and it requires a well-established routine. It may take days, but it is also normal if it takes months to teach your pup where its drop zone is and how to control itself until it gets there. It will also require a lot of directions, as your puppy cannot read your mind. Even if it is house trained, you will still need to direct it and tell it what you want it to do. And finally, you will need to be consistent: where you will take it and when, what its behavioral signs are, and what your route will be like, are all factors that you have to consider (and stick to!) if you want to be successful.

Time + direction + consistency is the secret formula that will help you potty train your pooch.

Steps to Potty Training

Step #1: Understand Your Puppy's Breed Behavior and Needs

Not all dogs have the same needs. Before you get discouraged by your training failure, see what you have been doing wrong. Each breed has its unique needs or may also have special behavior that requires a different approach. For instance, if your dog is of a small breed such as Chihuahua, you should keep in mind that their small bladder will require them to urinate much more frequently than Bulldogs, for instance. Also, with smaller breeds, accidents are more likely to happen, even if your puppy is successfully house trained. So keep that in mind when establishing a routine.

Step #2: Choose a Potty Zone

Choosing a drop zone for your pup and teaching your puppy that that's the place where it can safely eliminate waste is of extreme importance, not only for you to have a well-behaved dog with healthy habits, but also to prevent your house from becoming an unsanitary environment.

But, how do you pick the right potty zone and what should you have in mind while doing so? Now, this really depends on your free time, needs, and personal preferences. The most important thing is for your puppy's bathroom area to be easy to clean and not visited by other dogs.

If your puppy is still young and hasn't received all of the necessary vaccines yet, it is recommended that you avoid areas that are too public, such as parks. Talk to your puppy's veterinarian and ask for their advice.

Step #3: Attach Leash and Accompany

Even if the drop zone is in your own backyard, a few feet away from your house, until your pup is trained enough to understand the whole concept of potty runs, you will have to accompany it to its bathroom area. Your pooch will also have to be leashed in order for you to be able to take it to the drop zone.

Step #4: Blaze the Trail

Most dog owners fail to potty train their puppies with success because they make one giant mistake – they do not follow the same path to the drop zone. Your puppy is extremely adaptive. It is a fast learner with a great memory. To make the process a lot easier, choose the same path to its potty area, at least until it is fully house trained. That means for you to go out through the same door, making the same turn, using the same bush, etc.

Another important thing is to never carry your pup to the drop zone, no matter how small (or slow) it may be. Your pup needs to be leashed and to walk on its own in order to learn how to navigate the path on its own.

Step #5: Use the Command Word Right

In order for you to be able to train your puppy to eliminate waste on cue, you will not only need to come up with a good command word, but you will also need to use it right. For instance, if you say "Go" when you reach the drop zone but your puppy is not showing any sign of being ready to urinate, you are only diminishing the power of the word. If you want your pup to understand what "Go" or "Get Busy" or whatever command word you choose means, you need to use it whilst the dog is eliminating waste.

So, once you get to the drop zone, stand still. Do not move and do not interact. Simply wait for your puppy to do its business as soon as you see it relieving itself, firmly say the command word. Repeat every time, for as long as it takes for your pup to learn, eventually (usually after a month or so), your pooch will be able to go on cue.

Step #6: Praise and Reward

Once your pup eliminates waste, praise it immediately. Say "Good Boy" or whatever praise word you have chosen and reward it with a tasty treat. This will help your pooch associate eliminating waste with praise and reward, kick-starting the potty-training process, and helping it learn quicker.

Establishing a Potty Schedule

Potty training your pup may seem like a lot of work, but once you are able to determine when your pup needs to go, it will be a lot easier for you. Of course, there is the previously mentioned eat-drink-rest-play-chew routine, but unless you know approximately how many times a day your pup needs to go potty, all of the behavior-tracking and taking-notes process will have very little meaning.

Well, exactly how many potty breaks does your puppy need? In the beginning, keep in mind that you will have to take your pooch outside every hour or two, as very young puppies need to go more frequently.

Here are some general guidelines that can help you with potty training:

<u>6 to 14 Weeks</u> – 8 to 10 times a day

<u>14 to 20 Weeks</u> – 6 to 8 times a day

<u>20 to 30 Weeks</u> – 4 to 6 times a day

<u>30 Weeks and Older</u> – 3 to 4 times a day

Based on the guidelines above, your pup's breed, as well as its unique condition, you need to set up a potty schedule.

Here is an example that a dog owner who works outside of their home can use:

Early Morning - Go Outside

Breakfast – Go Outside after Breakfast

Lunch Break Feeding – Go Outside

Midafternoon – Young Puppies Should Go Outside

Home from Work – Go Outside

Dinnertime (between 5 and 6 pm) – Go Outside

7:30 p.m. – Remove Puppy's Water

Before Going to Bed – Go Outside

Middle of the Night – Go Outside, if necessary

Keep in mind that your pup needs regular exercise, so if your work prevents you from providing that, consider hiring a dog walker. Just make sure to let your walker know your rules and schedule, in order to keep the training process on the right track.

Potty When Alone

The schedule above is a great example of how you can organize the potty breaks, but if you think that it's a magic bullet that will help your pup to hold it in while you're gone, you are so wrong. Remember, the puppy's bladder is a muscle that develops last. It fills up very fast, and before your pooch reaches social maturity, which happens around month 5, your puppy will have the urge to go a lot more than you probably want it to. Asking your pup to wait a while until you get back from work is just not going to happen.

If you cannot find a good solution for this, you can consider purchasing a playpen for your pooch. Let the playpen be for alone time for your puppy where it can both, sleep, and eliminate waste. Have a playpen that is large enough for your pooch to sleep in on one side and go potty on the other side.

First, make sure that that the playpen is made of a material that is non-absorbent and that is easy to clean. Place your pup's bedding and toys on one end of the playpen. Cover the remaining space with absorbent pads where your pup can go potty. Chances are, your pooch will eliminate on the pads, which can be quite handy.

The minute you get home, take your pup outside. Do not offer access to the playpen when you are home. Also, do not use the crate for this purpose. You need to teach your pup that the crate is for sleeping and resting only. If you encourage eliminating waste there, you will never be able to get it back on the right track again.

Use this technique for the first few weeks, if the pup needs to go potty more times than you can take him outside. Once it matures a bit and can control its urge better, you should stop putting it in the playpen. Crate him regularly instead.

Handling Accidents the Right Way

You have a small puppy in your home – messy carpets and potty accidents are pretty much part of the deal. It will be a while until your puppy is fully house trained and mature enough to control its urge to go. Smelly accidents are inevitable, but how you approach these situations can also have a huge impact on how successful the house training process will be.

When you catch your young puppy in the act of eliminating waste, the best approach is to try to take its mind off of it:

1. When you see your puppy relieving itself on the floor, startle it immediately. Saying "Ep, ep", jumping up and down, or clapping your hands may do the trick.

2. Once your pooch is interrupted, attach its leash and take it to its drop zone immediately. Now, your pup may not have the need to go now since it has probably already eliminated on the floor, but that's not really the point here. What's important is to teach your puppy that urinating or defecating in the house is not allowed and that its drop zone is the safe place to do it.

3. If your pup manages to relieve itself, however, praise it like crazy for being good, and reward it immediately.

Keep in mind that you need to startle, but not scare your pup when you catch it in the act. The intent is to get your puppy's immediate attention. To help it understand and remember that what it is doing is wrong, it is recommended for you to use the same word, catchphrase, or make the same noise every time.

Do not punish your pup for eliminating inside. The old book says you should make it sniff its urine and slap it on the nose with a rolled newspaper, but besides being cruel, this can have a counter effect. In that situation, your puppy will only learn that it's unacceptable to eliminate waste and will most likely try to do it somewhere where you cannot reach easily so that it won't get punished again.

Tips for Successful Potty Training

Here are some tips that can help you potty train your pup better and faster:

<u>Watch the Water Intake</u> – Young puppies drink more water if they are bored or nervous. Make sure your pup gets enough exercise, and monitor its water intake closely. Give it access to its water bowl around meal times and when you believe it is thirsty.

Remove its water bowl after 7:30 p.m. If your pooch wants to have a drink after that, give it a small amount, no more than half a cup, or even better, give it a few ice cubes for it to play with and keep thirst at bay.

Limit its water intake to prevent excessive urination, however, be careful not to dehydrate your puppy. If it is panting or becoming lethargic, offer it its water bowl immediately.

<u>Lay off the Treats</u> – The treats play a huge part in training your puppy with positive reinforcement, however that doesn't mean that you should give them sporadically throughout the whole day. If you treat your pooch more than you should, it will most likely start pooping a lot more in the house, and its habits for elimination will become random.

Try to give smaller treats and reward only when training, if possible.

<u>Clean Up the Accidents Privately</u> – It is a mistake for you to let your puppy see you clean up its elimination accidents. That way you send it the wrong signals and you are almost encouraging that action by offering it a nurturing-like acceptance. When your puppy makes a mess, take it to another room or isolate it until you get the mess all cleaned up.

<u>Neutralize the Odor</u> – It is a common knowledge that dogs have a very strong sense of smell. Being an excellent sniffer, your pup will most likely return to eliminate waste where the smell of its urine is concentrated. Even if you cannot sense it, yes. For that purpose, make sure to always neutralize the odor of your pup's urine after an accident. Purchase an odor neutralizer from your nearest pet store, or even make your own solution by mixing an equal amount of water and vinegar and adding a few drops of essential oils to it. Place it in a spray bottle and, after cleaning, spray the area where the puppy has eliminated waste, to neutralize the smell.

Training Through Puppy's Growth Stages

Now, let's turn you into a proper trainer. This chapter is what you have signed up for when hitting the "buy now" button. It covers the basic directions and teaches the commands that puppies must learn in order to feel like an integrated part of the human world. Through the power of the word, you will be able to establish a communication bond like no other. Training your puppy is not just about turning it into an obedient dog. It's also about fostering mutual understanding for a lasting relationship.

Depending on the dog type, as well as the unique personality of your puppy, the training process can either be short and super effective or it may require some extra effort. Once you begin the practice, you will also learn that some commands are a breeze to teach while others have to be repeated dozens of times. Do not fret! Approach the training with the thought that you are actually teaching English words to another species. A certain amount of patience is indeed required.

The training sessions are divided and organized with the growth stages of your puppy in mind, for your convenience. From its early infant stages guiding you all the way to its adulthood, this chapter will help you master the basic commands and teach your puppy order and discipline with love.

8 to 12 Weeks

After the weaning period is over, which happens somewhere around week 7, your puppy is ready to be socialized and introduced to your family. If you still haven't adopted your puppy, make sure to do it when it has reached its 8th week. The weaning period is extremely important for baby puppies not only because the mother provides essential antibodies that will protect the puppy's health for many weeks to come, but also because those pups that stay with their mother throughout this period learn the doggy language and bite inhibition much better. If your puppy has been separated from its canine family way too early, it may be much more insecure around its new human family.

After your puppy is introduced with your family, it is only natural to want to teach it basic directions and train it to be disciplined. However, keep in in mind that the period before the 12th week is called the *infant period* for a reason. Your pup is just like an infant baby. It may be capable to learn a few things here and there, but its brain is not fully developed yet. That being said, don't expect too much from a puppy that's not 12 weeks old. You can start with the basic stuff but keep your expectations low.

Say Its Name

Your puppy may not be ready for some more advanced training sessions yet, but it's definitely never too early to start teaching it its own name. Use its name as often as you possibly can. When playing with it, when offering it a treat, or when you are simply praising or petting it. If you want to, you can also use a nickname that will highlight the cheerful moments and help your puppy associate its name with your positive attention. This can help you later on during the training process, as hearing its name will mean spending some fun time with you.

Just make sure to use a sharp but positive tone when calling to your puppy. Avoid sing-songs or speaking gibberish to your puppy just because it is a cuddly little thing. It may be just an infant and cannot fully grasp what's going on around it, but this is the perfect time for you to set the training basis. If you fail to teach your puppy how to respond to its name the minute you bring it home, you will need to work harder later on.

Get Them Used to the Leash

It is too early for you to introduce your puppy to the wonders of the dog park or the nearest beach. But just because you cannot take it for a walk around your neighborhood doesn't mean that you shouldn't get it used to the leash.

Put the collar on your puppy immediately after you bring it home. It will most likely fuss at first, but that's okay. Eventually, it will get used to it. If it has trouble accepting it, try the exercise from Chapter 5. Once it is comfortable with wearing its collar around its neck, it is time for you to attach the leash on it. Let it drag it around for a day until it gets used to it. After a day or so, you can pick up the leash and follow it around. As it becomes comfortable with you following it around, you can start calling its name and begin encouraging it to follow you.

If your pup is not particularly interested in strolling around your living room with you, try to do something to gain your puppy's interest. Foolish things always seem to do the trick. When it responds and begins following you, quickly say *"Follow"* and praise it by kneeling to offer a hug.

If it is too stubborn to accept the leash and collar, do not despair. Maybe your pup is just not ready at this stage. Keep in mind that your puppy is not 12 weeks old yet. Do not push it too hard. Drop everything and give it a try another day.

"Sit" and "Okay"

Although this stage is best for cuddling and spending quality time with your cute pooch, that doesn't mean that you cannot lay out the training basis. And working on simple commands such as *sit* and *okay* makes the perfect training foundation:

Grab a treat in your hand and show it to your puppy. It will probably get too excited and jumpy. That's okay. Do not force it into anything. Just slowly lower the hand with the treat to the floor, to see if you can lure it into a sitting-position. As you are lowering the hand, firmly say **"Sit"**.

1. Most puppies will most likely just lower their heads. See if you can use your other hand to gently show your puppy what it is supposed to do. Be careful, do not push, squeeze, or press too hard. Simply position your puppy by touching its waist muscles below its ribs so your puppy will know that it is supposed to sit.

2. This may take longer than expected, and that's perfectly okay. Keep in mind that you are trying to teach a baby to sit. Be patient and do not despair if your pup cannot quite figure out what is expected of him. If it manages to sit down, give it the treat immediately, as a reward.

Do not expect too much from the "Sit" command just yet. Introduce it just to help your pup accept the training routine easier. You can start training your puppy to sit much more intensively, once it is at least 12 weeks old.

The infant period is the perfect time for you to start using a happy and encouraging word. Most trainers choose "Okay" as a positive command to give their pup permission, however, "Good Boy/Girl" or any other positive word of choice will do just fine. Help your puppy associate this command with good behavior and positive things. For instance, when it sits down on its own, say **"Okay"**. When it takes your treat or starts eating its meal, repeat this command. Give it a toy and say **"Okay"** just before it starts chewing on it, to help it understand that saying this positive command means giving it permission to complete what's on its mind.

Walking the Stairs

Stairs are known to probably be the most intimidating obstacle that young puppies are faced with. This is especially the case with smaller breeds that just aren't built to tackle the stairs just yet. Even if you have a bigger puppy that can walk up and down the stairs at this stage, keep in mind that most young puppies have a type of *stair phobia* as they are too young to determine just how much they can and cannot handle, as their depth perception has yet to be developed.

If you have stairs in your home, this is the perfect time for you to start encouraging your puppy to use them. Lower yourself to its position and gently cradle its belly while guiding its paws up and down the stairs. If even this is too frightening for your puppy, have another family member cheer your pooch from a few stairs away, to give it the encouragement to start moving its paws more freely.

Handling

Fear is a common occurrence in puppies that haven't reached 12 weeks of age. In fact, most trainers refer to the '8-12 weeks' stage as the *fear imprint period*. Fears and unpleasant experiences that occur before the 12th week seem to leave a much more lasting impression on puppies. Young puppies are often afraid of humans. If you fail to provide proper handling, your puppy may grow into a fearful dog that is wary of people.

Handling is a very important part that you as a puppy owner should take care of immediately after bringing your puppy home. This will not only help your pooch accept you much faster and jumpstart the training method, but it will also be much appreciated during veterinarian visits.

Handling can be done only when your puppy is calmed. Do not by any chance try to force handle, as that will have a counter effect. Instead, lay down on the floor with your puppy and as you are calmly petting it, perform a routine check-up. Peek into its ears, hold its head gently and look deeply into its eyes, handle its paws like you are trimming the nails, touch the base of your puppy's tail, and press the belly gently. Playing veterinarian will not only be fun, but it will also get your pup used to the human touch and become unafraid of handling.

To avoid scaring your puppy, praise it with hugs and reward with treats while handling it.

Socializing

Puppies at this age shouldn't be taken outside for a walk, but that doesn't mean that they cannot be introduced to your close friends and family. The period before the 12th week is the perfect time for you to begin the socialization process, as that will help your pooch adapt to new people and unfamiliar situations easily. So, in order to help your puppy, grow into a confident and well-adjusted dog that is comfortable around people and other dogs, you will need to expose it to strangers as early as possible.

Invite your friends and neighbors over (if you can invite some active kids over that would be perfect) or if possible, have a play date with another healthy dog. The important thing about early socialization is to help your pup build confidence and become familiar with uncertainties. Ask your guests to offer treats and handle your puppy gently in order for your pup to be as comfortable as possible. Have it near you at all times to keep the discomfort at a minimum., and to let it know that you are always by its side. When people approach your puppy and want to pet it, take advantage of the "Sit" command and encourage it to be calm while bracing it into a sitting position gently and giving it its favorite treat afterward.

Practice Food Conditioning

It is in a puppy's nature to protect what's theirs, so do not be surprised if your pooch develops a food or object guarding habit. Most puppies guard their food bowls or their toys and objects from other dogs but know that your pup can be just as defensive to your approach as well.

However, if you start with early food conditioning, you can prevent this mindset and eradicate food guarding from your pup's development.

1. Every other day when your pup is having a meal, go to it.

2. Offer it a biscuit or another doggy treat when it is halfway finished with its meal. Pat it on the head and say **"Good Boy/Girl"** or **"Okay"**.

3. When it accepts the treat, slowly take the food bowl away from it. Make sure to do this while your pup is still eating the biscuit.

4. After it has finished eating the treat, wait 10-15 seconds before returning the food bowl to it. Pat it on the head, and give it the **"Okay"** command again.

Make sure to involve all family members in this exercise, especially if there are children in the house. Food conditioning should be executed by everyone who shares the same roof with your puppy in order to avoid your pup developing the need to guard and protect its belongings from others.

12 to 16 Weeks

If you have a child, then you know that the second year of their life is called *terrible twos* for a reason. They become sneaky little creatures, using your weaknesses to their advantage. But what you probably didn't know is that the second puppy growth stage (the infant period doesn't count) also shares the same name.

During this, terrible second phase, your pooch is starting to realize what behaviors get your attention, what gets it the yummiest treats, and who is the boss. And yes, in your puppy's eyes, you may not be the person in charge. It may be your four-year-old daughter who gives it biscuits when no one's looking.

Even though you may think that your puppy is confident and pretty independent, the truth is, your puppy craves direction. If you let your pup run around without correcting misbehavior and teaching the right way, you will have a lot on your hands later on. The tips and tricks in this section will help you teach basic commands to a 12-month old puppy and guide your pooch through this terrible and pretty insecure period.

Keeping the Control

Giving your puppy complete freedom just because it is indoors is a terrible mistake. Being free to do whatever it wants means misbehavior, and misbehavior results in you paying for it – literally, by fixing broken furniture, and by investing more time and effort in future training.

Not to mention that an unsupervised puppy can be a danger to itself. Because, let's face it, no matter how doggy-proofed your house may be, your puppy will always find a choking hazard to chew on.

Keep in mind that your puppy is still pretty young, so you have to have your eyes on it most of the time. Here are some tips on how to keep your pup near you:

- Let it sit in an enclosed area where you can observe it easily. A gated kitchen is just one example.

- If you have bought a special crate of the right size for your puppy, you can keep it there whenever you cannot keep your eyes on it. Just remember to give it some toys to chew on, to keep boredom at bay.

- Make sure it is near you all the time, by attaching it to a leash. If you are dealing with a super active puppy that cannot be calmed that easily, then perhaps attaching it to a dragging lead will help you keep a constant eye on your puppy.

Just remember to praise and treat your puppy whenever it is confined, to encourage good behavior.

The TEN Basics

It may seem to you like your puppy understands nothing but food and chewing on chairs, but at this stage, your pooch has the capacity of having a ten-word vocabulary. Think of your puppy now as a toddler who can absorb knowledge but only if it interests them. It can learn a lot at this stage, but your bundle of joy is very much vulnerable to your impressions. Before we start with the ten basics, let's make sure you know how to start the training process the right way:

- Stay cool. Even if you have to repeat a single command dozens of times, do not get frustrated, or at least, don't let your pup see it. If you get impatient, that will only scare your puppy which will make it lose interest and become less responsive to the training sessions.

- Give clear and single directions. Be firm and make sure to enunciate the syllables. Repeat the command once, with the right tone and level of firmness. Keep in mind that a firm DOWN sounds a lot different than down-down-down-oh-come-on-puppy-please-get-down.

- Keep in mind that the pup is still very young, so give the directions when the puppy is in the right mood, which is usually during playtime and when your puppy is not hungry.

- Use your hands to signal and give visual directions if needed.

- Do not forget to immediately reward the pup after completing the task.

#1: Buddy's Name

The very first word that most puppies learn is their name. If you have already managed to get your puppy to come to you or react when it hears its name, you can check this off your list. But if your pooch is too stubborn or lazy to cooperate, you may need to teach it that when you say your puppy's name, that means "I am talking to you and I want you to pay attention".

When you call your pup by its name, it should be a cue for them to drop everything, turn towards you, and give you its full attention. If your pup is not quite responsive, it might be because you have been using its name the wrong way. The puppy's name should have one single meaning – attention. If you are using it as a correction or you are shouting it in an angry tone when you get mad at them, you are sending it confusing signals. To your pup, its name might mean three things:

1. Come to me now and give me your attention.
2. You are being very naughty and I am telling you off.
3. Come now, boy/girl. No? Now, I am angry.

Before you can actually teach your pup to respond whenever it hears its name, you need to first stop associating with negative things. Otherwise, you are only confusing your dog and making it harder for it to determine how it should respond to the sound of its name.

Step 1: Get Buddy's Attention

Before you begin, make sure that it is just you, your puppy, and a bag of treats. In order for it to learn, you need to make sure that there isn't anything that can distract it. Now, say its name in a warm tone, but make it sound firm. If you get no response, say it again, but this time, clap your hands or do a kissing noise to get its attention.

Step 2: Reward Immediately!

As soon as your puppy gives you its attention, mark the desired behavior with a positive word. You can use **"Good Boy/Girl", "Okay", "Yes",** or whatever works for you. The important thing is to <u>tell</u> your pup that it has done something good. Immediately after saying the word, give your pup a treat to reward its good behavior.

Step 3: Repeat

Repeat this for as long as it takes until your puppy is able to give you its full attention no matter what. To do so, you first need to get its attention when it is not distracted, and gradually increase the distractions to make sure that your pup will be responsive even in the most distracting situations. Toys and biscuits are perfect distractions. Try to give it access to some, and then start with step 1 and step 2.

#2: Look Up!

Whether you manage to get your puppy to look at you when it is preoccupied with something else or not, in the most distracting situations, you will need more than just a glance. You will need to get your puppy to pause whatever it is doing and really focus on you. This is how you can train it to pay a bit more attention when you need it to:

1. Pick a moment when your pup is not tired, not hungry, and when there aren't too many distractions around.

2. Grab its favorite toy or a treat that you know it loves.

3. Stand above and call your puppy's name as you lift the toy or treat upwards, from its eyes to yours.

4. Keep the toy or treat in that position for 2 seconds.

5. Say a positive word such as **"Good Boy/Girl"** to mark the behavior, and then give it a treat as a reward.

6. Make a small pause and then repeat this exercise, only this time, keep the toy/treat near your eyes for 5 seconds. Mark, reward, and then repeat again. With each repetition, increase the time it must stare at you (from 2 to 10 seconds).

This exercise will train your puppy to give you more than a second of its attention when it becomes distracted.

#3: Follow!

Training your puppy to follow you is one of the first and most basics commands that your pooch should learn. In the beginning, it is recommended that you do this on the go, meaning that you should try to instill a habit to *follow* when you are walking your pup on the leash:

1. Fill your pocket with doggy treats.

2. Attach the puppy's leash to his collar.

3. As soon as you take the first step, say the word **"Follow"** in a firm, but friendly way.

4. If your puppy starts walking alongside you, mark the behavior and give it a treat. If it isn't too enthusiastic about it, see if you can encourage it by showing it the treat.

5. Encourage your puppy to follow you with treats, while saying the command **"Follow"** every couple of seconds.

6. Once it begins cooperating, start increasing the length between the treats.

Once you get your puppy to follow you when on the leash, you need to take this training session a step further and get your puppy to learn that follow should mean follow, even if there is no leash involved:

1. When the leash is not attached to your puppy, fill a treat cup with treats and show it to them.

2. Start walking and immediately say the word **"Follow"**.

3. If your pooch starts walking towards you, give them a single treat when it comes to you. If it is not too excited, shake the treat cup to try to boost their enthusiasm.

4. Again, repeat this a couple of times and lengthen the distance between the treats.

In most cases, this exercise works like a charm, and most puppies are able to learn the "Follow" command in a relatively short amount of time. However, it is not uncommon for dog owners to stumble upon resistance. If your puppy doesn't want to move even after being lured with treats, it is important for you to be able to keep your cool. Do not be tempted to drag them. Besides the fact that it can cause physical discomfort, it can also scare them and make the whole process a lot harder. Persuading them to follow you is also not an option as by doing so you will be only be reinforcing their resistance. Instead, what you should do, is get creative. What interests your pup the most? Jump around, squeak a toy, kneel down, or do something that you think will be able to encourage your puppy to follow you.

#4: Sit

"Sit" is probably the biggest sign that the puppy is well-behaved. Like a child that knows how to say "Please" when asking for something. It is one of the best dog's manners, and it lasts a lifetime. Teaching puppies to sit is also one of the most basic commands, and it is a lesson that most puppies master in no time. Here is a simple exercise that if done properly a couple of times a day, it can be easily taught in just 4 days:

1. Grab a couple of treats in your hand.

2. Bring your hand slowly to your puppy's nose. Allow them to sniff it just to realize what you are holding, but do not give them the treats just yet.

3. Put one of the treats between your thumb and index finger.

4. Say **"Sit"** as you bring the treat above the puppy's nose, about an inch or so apart. Move the treat hand so you can lure them into a sitting position.

5. Once your pup is seated, mark the good behavior by saying **"Okay"** or **"Good Boy/Girl"** and give them the treat.

6. Repeat this exercise until there are no more treats left in your hand.

Keep in mind that in order for this to work, the treat has to be placed just about an inch apart and kept right above the nose. Why is this important? Because if you hold your hand too high, your puppy will be encouraged to jump, and if you keep it too low, they will most likely just take it and not even try to sit down. Above the nose, and an inch apart is a perfect position.

As easy as teaching this command may seem, with some puppies, you may need a more 'manual' approach. If your puppy doesn't want to sit down and refuses to cooperate at all, you need to help it understand what is asked of them and physically get it into a sitting position:

1. Have your puppy on your left side, both of you facing the same direction.

2. Kneel down. If your puppy is of a smaller breed, you can place it on a chair or table for your convenience.

3. Place your right hand against its chest and your left one on the pup's shoulders.

4. Firmly say **"Sit"** and gently run your left hand over your puppy's shoulder, putting enough pressure to get them in a sitting position. By doing so, you will get your pup to sit on your hand.

5. When it is finally sitting on your hand, praise it with **"Good Boy/Girl"** and immediately give it a treat.

6. Repeat this exercise a couple of times, twice a day, for about 4 days.

#5: Down

"Down" is one of those ultimate cues. It literally means "Stop whatever it is you are doing this instant and lay down". This command can be a real life-saver when having guests over, especially if you are dealing with an overly cheerful and jumpy pup.

Introduce the "Down" command after your pup can sit when asked to, as this training session requires the puppy to know how to sit down on command.

This may be a bit trickier than "Sit", but "Down" can be mastered just as fast. Simply follow the steps below:

1. Take your puppy aside and grab some treats in your hand.

2. Instruct your pup to sit down. If you are still using the treats to lure it into a sitting position, it is best to leave teaching the "Down" command for after your pup learns to sit down without being tricked into that position.

3. Once your puppy is sitting on the floor, drop your treats on the floor, close to its paws, and immediately cover them with your hand.

4. Wait for a second to see the pup's reaction. If your puppy lays down on their own, say **"Down"** the second it gets down, and give it one of the treats immediately.

5. Repeat these steps until there are no more treats left. Do this exercise for as long as it takes until your puppy learns how to get down when told.

If your puppy gets down on its own, you are one lucky dog owner, as most pups struggle with this exercise and need some assistance. If your pup is unsure what it is supposed to do, you may need to get them into a "Down" position yourself:

1. Just press them gently between their shoulder blades to get them into this position. While doing that, say **"Down"** firmly.

2. Once your puppy's elbows hit the floor, mark the good behavior by saying **"Good Boy/Girl"** or **"Okay"** or whatever positive cue you have chosen, and give them a treat immediately.

3. Repeat this a couple of times until your puppy learns that it is supposed to get down on its own. Then, you can follow the steps from above.

6: Stand

There are times when this cue will be deeply appreciated. Imagine you have just gotten back from outside and your puppy's paws are all muddy. If your pup knows what "Stand" means, you will have no trouble wiping dirt off your pooch's paws. Not to mention that grooming will be a breeze.

Here is how you can teach your puppy to stand:

1. Grab a doggy treat and place it between your thumb and index finger.

2. Place the treat about an inch apart from your puppy's nose.

3. Say **"Stand"** firmly, and immediately lift your hand up as if you were pulling a string from your puppy's nose.

4. Once your puppy is standing, start cradling its belly with your hand as you repeat **"Stand"**. This will teach your pooch that "Stand" means getting into that position and staying there until it is told otherwise.

5. Make a 2-second pause and then say **"Okay"** or **"Good Boy/Girl"** to praise the good behavior, while giving them their reward – the yummy treat – immediately.

6. Repeat these steps with a couple of treats, a few times a day.

Now, in the ideal scenario, your puppy will be able to stand and hold that position for as long as the treat is in front of them. But, in most cases, young pups are impatient and try to snatch the treat from your hand. If your puppy is like that, just make sure to hold the treat firmly, and use a cue that will discourage them such as **"Ep, ep"**. Dealing with an impatient pup may require some extra effort, but the steps from above will surely help you teach your pooch to stand.

#7: Give

Puppies at this stage are just like two-year-olds. They love to play with toys, but the whole concept of sharing is not familiar to them. It is your job to teach your puppy that it is supposed to share. Mastering this command will be especially appreciated when your pooch finds something dangerous to chew on when out for a walk.

Here is how you can teach your puppy to give:

1. Find a toy that your puppy likes to play with and have it near you. Put a couple of doggy treats in your pocket, as well.

2. Kneel down on the floor and spend a minute or two praising your pooch and petting it happily, before you bring out its toy.

3. Now, take its toy, toss it in the air, and catch it yourself. This is done so you can pique your puppy's interest and make them want to play.

4. Then, toss it again, only this time, give it just a short toss so that your puppy can catch it.

5. If your pup takes the toy, let them have it for a minute or two. Do not try to take it away from them immediately, as it is important for them to feel that you're not challenging them.

6. Now that it has had its fun, bring out the doggy treat. As you offer it the treat, it is supposed to spit out its squeaky toy and take it. As it does that, firmly say **"Give"** and take the toy with your hand.

7. Praise them by saying **"Good Boy/Girl"** or **"Okay"**.

8. Once it has eaten the treat, give it back its toy. This is very important, as it will highlight your good intention. Otherwise, your pup may associate this action with you stealing their possessions.

9. Repeat steps 4,5,6, and 7 until your puppy understands the game. If it looks at you immediately after it picks up his toy, that means that it is ready to "Give".

There are a couple of things that may cause you trouble with this exercise:

1. First, your puppy may run away from you the second it sinks its teeth into the toy and try to get its squeaky friend to the nearest corner. If that is the case, try again, but this time, keep your puppy on a short leash.

2. The other thing that can be tricky, is if your puppy simply refuses to release the toy. When that happens, simply squeeze their upper muzzle, behind their canine teeth. Once it releases the toy, praise them and reward as usual. The point is for your puppy to understand how to play this game and learn that "Give" means releasing.

#8: Settle Down

The period between 12 and 16 weeks is the perfect time for you to teach your puppy to settle down and go rest in their specially designated area. Just make sure that your puppy is actually older than 12 weeks, in order to avoid them feeling entrapped and insecure, as they cannot fully grasp the "Settle Down" concept during the fear imprint period.

Ideally, your pup should have a corner of its own in each room. And even more ideally, you should be able to direct them to that area when you are, for instance, having guests over, eating dinner, or you simply want them out of the way.

1. Attach your puppy's leash to its collar, grab the leash in your hand, and firmly say **"Settle Down"**, while pointing to the designated area with your other hand.

2. Now, since it will actually need the escort, take it to its spot where there will be a chewy toy waiting for it.

3. Stay there until it lays down and takes the toy.

4. Praise them and immediately give them a treat.

5. Do this in every room in your house, to make sure that your puppy understands that settling down means going to the nearest corner to rest.

Make sure not to leave treats instead of toys in his special spots, as they may mistakenly think that you only want them to eat the treats.

This exercise may take longer if you are dealing with a stubborn pup, but do not lose faith. Just be sure to leave a toy or another object that your pooch really enjoys chewing on, to speed up the process.

#9: Wait (and Okay)

The best way to teach your pup to wait is to use a door for this exercise. It is best to do this with treats and an interior door, but if you live in a house that has a yard, you can also use the front door and the access to outdoors as a reward (or combine it with a yummy treat).

1. Grab a few doggy treats and take your dog with you in the room.
2. Close the door and spend a minute or two with the puppy inside the room. However, do not play games or get them too excited as you need your puppy to be calm for this exercise.
3. Walk to the door, as you usually do. When your puppy comes along, firmly say **"Wait"**.
4. Now, place your hand on the doorknob. Chances are, your pup will start impatiently dancing around and getting between your legs.
5. Open the door, but not more than a crack. If the puppy pushes to go through, say **"No"**, **"Whoops"**, or whatever cue you want to use to let your pup know that it is not supposed to go first.
6. Close the door and go a few steps back. Wait for a moment.
7. When your pup makes eye contact, go to the door again, and say **"Wait"** again. When your puppy moves forward, tell them **"No"** again, and shut the door.
8. Wait for them to get calm. Then, reach for the door again, but only if your pup remains calm. Repeat the process again. If it stays behind you and waits, give them the release command **"Okay"**, and let them step outside.

The point of this exercise is to practice patience and get your puppy to wait when you need them to. To achieve that, you will need to gradually increase the waiting time with each subsequent exercise.

If this doesn't work, you can try luring them with a treat:

1. Grab a treat, go inside a room, and close the door.

2. Crack the door open and say **"Wait"** while holding your treat hand behind your back, so that your puppy stays behind you.

3. Keep your hand there for a couple of seconds, then slowly move it towards the door, while saying **"Okay"**.

4. Let them leave the room, then praise them immediately, and reward them with the treat.

Keep in mind that in order for your pooch to learn the "Wait" command, you will have to be able to do it without luring them with treats. Repeat this exercise for as long as it takes for your puppy to understand what the treat is there for, and then give the previous exercise a try, to practice "Wait" and "Okay" with your puppy without the luring technique.

#10: Excuse Me

"Excuse me" may not be the most basic command, to be honest, but this is the best time to teach your pup to be careful not to get in your way. Because young pups love doing that. As soon as they figure out that blocking your way gets them attention, they start doing it in order to steal some cuddling time from you. They don't care if your arms are full of grocery bags or that you're carrying a heavy laundry basket, and they surely cannot realize that they can trip you up, or even worse, that they can get stepped on.

In order for you to prevent that from happing, a simple verbal cue is used from the 12th week, so that your puppy can learn how to back up politely and respect your space. If you have an older dog, you can practice this exercise with luring treats, but to save yourself some time, as well as to help your puppy understand what it is supposed to do, teaching "Excuse me" to a 12-week-old pup is most effective if done physically:

1. Grab a few treats in your hand and have your puppy stand in front of you.

2. Shuffle your feet underneath their belly, firmly say **"Excuse Me"** and gently move them out of the way.

3. As soon as your puppy is out of your way, praise them with **"Good Boy/Girl"** and give them a treat.

4. Praise them for another minute or so, and then repeat this exercise again. Repeat a couple of times a day during this growth stage.

Handling and Socializing

This is probably the period during which you will begin taking your puppy outside. It will explore new sights and different places, but it will also be introduced to other living creatures. Do not forget that your pooch loves its two-legged and four-legged friends. Give them access to other puppies, bring them with you when going out for a walk with a friend, and make sure that it meets new faces almost every day. If you cannot do this on your own, ask your puppy's veterinarian to recommend you a puppy class where you can meet other well-managed canines, as well as people so that your puppy can spend some time around them.

Keep in mind that socialization plays a huge part in the puppy's growth and is especially important for the way it will grow to treat people. Frequent socialization doesn't create spoiled dogs, quite the contrary. It just makes them understand that your judgment, when people are concerned, is right, and prevents them from doing something stupid such as barking excessively, being aggressive, or even biting a stranger in the future.

During this period, handling your pup should also be an important part of the schedule. Make sure to regularly touch and check your pup's ears, tail and paws. If your puppy will also be around children, make sure they handle them as well. Your pup needs to get used to connecting with humans, so handling them regularly from the early stages is extremely important.

Teething

12 to 16 weeks is the time when your puppy's teeth will start to shred and fall out, in order for new, permanent teeth to emerge, so do not be surprised if you find white crumbs or rice-sized teeth all over your house.

A puppy's mouth is filled with 28 tiny teeth, and when your puppy is about three or four months old, these razor-sharp teeth will fall out and make room for 42 adult teeth. This period can be extremely painful for the puppy, as their gum will most likely be sore. If you have children, you are probably aware of how uncomfortable a teething baby can be.

Somewhere between the 12th and 16th week, your puppy's teeth will start falling out, and they will become irritated, uncomfortable, and more nervous. Besides offering comfort in the form of petting and spending quality time with them, you should also provide something to ease the pain. Offer quality chew toys and take them to a vet check in order to make sure that everything is progressing the way it should.

16 to 24 Weeks

Welcome to adolescence! This is the stage when you realize that just because your pup knows basic directions doesn't mean that it will be in the mood to respond to them. Some days may be livable, but others may be just too overwhelming. Your puppy will bolt, chase, and nip on pretty much everything mobile. It may bark at you annoyingly when you will not be in the mood to spend the whole afternoon chasing them around, or it may even mount you when it feels like it. At this stage, your pooch will crave attention more than ever. It desires to be the center of it, and good luck to you if you try to take the crown away from them.

Know that all that is perfectly normal. Just like with human adolescence, your puppy is now going through a pretty confusing period that you just have to endure patiently. It needs your guidance now more than ever, so be sure to remind yourself that their outbursts are a normal part of their development and that by not giving up on the training sessions, each day, you are a step closer to having a well-behaved and respectful friend for life.

Once your pooch turns 16 weeks, you should establish a strictly organized training routine that you (and your family members) should control closely. Whatever directions your pup has managed to master can be exercised throughout the whole day. Teaching new directions should be left for the time you've set aside for training your puppy only, as you need to keep them interested and responsive. Otherwise, your puppy may get overwhelmed way too soon, and you will end up investing a lot more effort into the training. Keep the sessions short, but upbeat and positive.

Allowing More Freedom

Even though your pup may seem to be a lot more responsive than 4 weeks ago, it still sees your entire house as a hidden treasure. The urge for digging, chewing, and tearing things apart is still uncontrollable to a great extent. Leaving your pup unattended is just like leaving your teenage son alone in the house for the whole weekend. It's trouble waiting to happen.

You should be able to keep a close eye on your puppy and have them in an enclosed area. When that's not possible, your puppy's free time in the house should still be controlled with a leash.

As your puppy's getting more obedient and the training progresses, you should start allowing more freedom around the house, gradually. Gate a larger area, let them play around unleashed for short periods of time and track their behavior. Don't rush it though. Keep in mind that your puppy is still young and overly excited, so don't think that it has mastered its obedience class ahead of time.

The FIVE Power Words

As soon as your pup learns the ten basic words, you need to start working on enriching its vocabulary. As your puppy is progressing both mentally and physically, you need to teach them five power words that are essential for your pooch's obedience training. Once it is able to master Heel, Stay, No, Come, and Stand-Stay, the afternoon walks in the park will become a real treat for you both.

Heel

Heel means "walk by my side nicely". It means showing your dog that pulling on the leash as you are walking along the street is not acceptable. This is probably the command that most dog owners are impatient for their puppies to master, as there is nothing more rewarding than having your pooch standing and walking calmly by your side. Sure, the heel is not the easiest thing to teach and it may need some time to synchronize, but once your pup gets a handle of it, you will be able to easily maneuver through a crowded park and even call your puppy to heel from a distance.

Introduce

It is recommended to start with the "heel" command inside your home for the first couple of days, as introducing this new command on one of your walks may contribute to diluting the power of the word.

1. Clear out a room and attach your puppy's leash to their collar. Place a few doggy treats inside your pocket.

2. Take the leash and relax your arm straight.

3. Firmly say **"Heel"** and immediately begin walking in a counterclockwise circle, with your puppy on the inside. Make sure to walk in a cheerful and upbeat manner. Keep your head high and keep your shoulders back to give the right message.

4. If your puppy starts walking with you, stop after making a circle by releasing with an **"Ok"**. Praise your pup immediately and give them a treat.

5. Then, place your pooch in a sitting position and repeat this for four more circles. Do this exercise twice a day.

Work on the Finish

If this sounds too miraculous for your pup's skills, don't worry. You are not the only one. In fact, most pups need quite a bit of training before they manage to learn what "heel" means, so don't despair if your pooch doesn't get it right from the start. Only a handful of pups actually do.

If your puppy is confused and does not get that they should stop when you do, you may need a trick to avoid them pulling on the leash:

Just as you are preparing to stop the circle slow down a bit, and lift your left foot high (just pretend that you are marching) and drop it on the floor very lightly. This action will give your pup a cue that it is supposed to slow down, stop, and end the circle by sitting down by your side.

Change the Pace

Don't be surprised if your pup doesn't (or doesn't want to) understand that you are slowing down. If it is still pulling on the leash, you may need to let them know that you are actually changing the pace:

Start the circle by trotting. Keep your leash hand behind the seam of your pants steady, but relaxed. Lengthen your stride to slow down the pace. Imagine that you are driving a car. Change the gear with a sound such as *Shh or Clk,* to help your pup realize the change.

Try a Different Approach

If the treat reward just doesn't seem to do the trick for your pup here, and it is still unaware of what the" heel" exercise is about, maybe luring them with a treat will help them understand that it is supposed to walk by your side:

1. Attach your puppy's leash to its collar, grab the leash with your left hand, and have a couple of doggy's treats in your right.

2. Keep your right hand by your side, close to their nose.

3. Say **"Heel"** as you start walking in a circle. Just like before, keep them on the inside.

4. If your pooch starts walking by your side, give them one of the treats, but do it on the go – do not stop just yet.

5. After the first circle is over, say **"Heel"** again, and again, give them a treat.

6. Make a few circles, depending on how many treats you are holding in your hand.

7. Release with the word **"Ok"**, stop, and immediately praise your puppy for their behavior.

Practice this command in your home only for now but vary the rooms and directions. Add some distractions gradually, such as having other people in the room, having the TV on, having their favorite toy on the floor, etc. Go between the chairs, around the kitchen island, the coffee table, etc.

The whole point of practicing this exercise in your home is to get the right level of enthusiasm in your voice, as well as to control the pup's position with the luring technique. Once you get rid of the luring treat - which should be done after a week or so after your pup understands the point of the exercise - you should still continue practicing in your home in order to teach your puppy how to flawlessly execute this command, so you can both handle heeling outside the comfort of your home.

Heeling in Public

After a couple of weeks of home training, you are ready to incorporate heel into your walks outside. Don't rush it though. In the beginning, tell your pup to heel after one-fourth of your walk. Keep it small, but increase the heeling distance over the next month, until Buddy has no trouble walking by your side.

Take heeling to another level by practicing it in more crowded situations such as in parking lots.

Keep in mind that in order for this to work, you need to stay calm. If you yell "Heel, heel, heel!", and start jerking your pooch around, it will become confused about the command, get excited to play, and you will only end up diluting the power that the word "Heel" should have. Instead, if it is not quite following you yet, ask yourself whether you are asking too much too soon, and take the exercise back to your backyard. Maybe your pooch simply needs more training before it can successfully handle heeling when strange distractions come his way.

No

In a perfect scenario, you should be able to tell your pup "No" whenever it is doing something that is undesirable, and it is supposed to drop everything without even showing a shred of resistance. It sounds almost miraculous, but you can actually train your pooch to look the other way when you say "No", even if the distraction is too hard to resist.

What Not to Do

In order for you to be able to teach your pup to understand the meaning of the word "No", first you need to understand how to use it properly. There are a couple of mistakes that most people make when teaching the "No" command. To avoid confusing your pooch, make sure NOT TO:

- <u>Shout It</u> – People usually shout the word "No", thinking that they are emphasizing its meaning that way. That is not the truth. By shouting the command, you are only adding fuel to the fire. Shouting to dogs sounds the same as barking to humans. It does not calm down the situation, but adds to the excitement.

- <u>Use It Repetitively</u> – Remember that "No, no, no, no" sounds different than a firm "No". Your pup may not be able to understand the command if you use it repetitively.

- <u>Use It with your puppy's Name</u> – Similarly to using it repetitively, using the command with your puppy's name is also confusing. In fact, most pups think that "No" is actually their second name. If you start using it with their name too often, it may associate this command with something positive (which its name is), and it will clearly have a counter effect.

- <u>Say It After the Action is Over</u> – If you say "No" to your puppy after the action has already been completed, it may not understand what you are upset at them for. Just think about it. Would you understand that I was angry at you for opening the can if I yelled at you after you drank the soda?

Teaching the Concept

Your puppy is still too young to teach them NO outdoors or to do it without the leash. It can be done, sure, but it will require a tremendous amount of effort from your side. The best and easiest way to teach them the NO concept is if you do it indoors, and if your puppy is leashed:

1. Attach the leash to their collar and stay with them in some room in your home.

2. Fill a treat cup and have it with you.

3. Have another family member hide a piece of cheese in another room.

4. Grab their leash and slowly start walking towards the cheese.

5. When they realize the cheese and gets too excited, firmly say **"No"** and immediately shake the treat cup to encourage them to turn their attention to you.

6. Once it is no longer staring at the cheese, but it is interested in what you have in your hand, praise them immediately and give them a single treat.

7. Go back to the other room and repeat the exercise again. The point is for your puppy to get the message that it is not supposed to touch the cheese when it hears you say "No".

Taking It Outside

Once your pup understands what "No" means, you can start incorporating this command into your walks. The best time to instruct this command is when you notice its ear antennas flicker. Firmly say **"No"** and even step away from the distraction in order to emphasize the meaning of the command. Don't forget to praise immediately and reward with a yummy doggy treat for encouragement.

Tip: If you have been using "Ep, ep" with your pup, you don't need to say "No" for minor distractions. Continue training but save this command for more important infractions. To correct when you catch him going astray (such as when sniffing something) just say "Ep, ep" instead.

Stay

When thinking about having a well-behaved puppy, most people are dreaming about mastering the "Stay" command. With the power of this word, you will be able to have your pooch seated for longer periods of time. Having the authority to instruct your puppy to stay when meeting someone, and prevent them from leaving their muddy paws all over that person, will be greatly appreciated.

But don't fool yourself into thinking that you can teach them this direction today and be able to make a ham sandwich in peace tomorrow. Just like with the previous commands, this direction should also be taught progressively.

Here are some rules you need to follow when teaching your pooch to "Stay":

- Do not look directly into your puppy's eyes; this will be too daunting for them. Instead, look over their head.

- When you start out, make sure that you are standing close to them, about 6 inches apart. If you create a longer distance in the beginning, the exercise may come off as scary to your pooch.

- Stand tall at all times. If you bend over, you will send you pooch the message that you're ready to play.

Here is how you can teach your puppy to stay:

1. Put a doggy treat in your puppy's food bowl. Hold the bowl with one of your hands.

2. In order for your pooch to be able to stay in a certain position, you must first instruct him to sit down. So, firmly instruct **"Sit"** while making a stop sign with your hand. Make sure to hold the hand in front of the puppy's nose.

3. The moment that your puppy sits down, say **"Stay"**.

4. Wait a few seconds to see how your pup will react. If it doesn't move, lower the bowl with treats.

5. Now, chances are, your pooch will disobey and will try to reach the treats. If that happens, take the bowl higher.

6. Repeat again. If it moves, take the bowl even higher. If not, lower it.

7. It's simple; whenever it obeys, lower the bowl. Whenever it misbehaves, you take the bowl higher and it is one step further from getting the treat. The exercise is over when you lower the bowl to the ground and allow them to get the treat. Just remember to praise them verbally when you do that, to let them know that you appreciate their good behavior.

The point of this exercise is to help your pooch understand that staying in place and not moving means getting the treats.

Come

If you ask me, "Come" is probably the trickiest command to teach, and in most cases, puppies cannot understand the true meaning of the word. Why? Because they have either gotten used to associating it with disobedience, or you have managed to poison the cue:

<u>Come as Disobedience</u> – The minute you bring your pup home, you start speaking with him and, believe it or not, teaching him your language. Even if you are not aware of it, your puppy already knows the word "Come", but in his head, it probably doesn't have the same meaning. If you have been chasing your pooch around the house, calling it to come to you desperately, or bribing it with yummy doggy delicacies, be sure that trouble is already brewing. Because your pup probably associates the word "Come" with disobedience or a round of a chasing game.

<u>Come as a Poisoned Cue</u> – If you have used the word "Come" to call out your dog and then did something that they would think of as negative, such as crating them, giving them a bath, or scolding them, that is poisoning the cue. In that case, your pooch is most likely afraid of the word "Come", because in their head, that means that something negative is about to happen.

It is your job to teach them that coming to you is a positive thing. You need to reformat the understanding that your puppy has towards this cue, just keep in mind that you will have to invest some effort, patience, and concentration. Do not expect immediate results, but try to repeat this exercise as often as possible in order to teach them good behavior.

The Right Approach

In order to avoid ending up disappointed, it is important for you to know that you cannot start with this training whenever you feel like it. In order for the lesson to be effective, you need to begin the training just when you are sure that your puppy will actually come when you instruct them to. Otherwise, "Come" will have no meaning. That is why you should train this command, only when your puppy is not preoccupied with other things and when you are sure that you can get their full attention:

1. Go to a clean area that is free of distractions. No TV, no other people, no cats, no toys, nothing.

2. Fill one of your hands with their favorite treats.

3. Make sure to stand a few feet apart from the pup. Let them notice the treat, and as it begins approaching you, firmly say **"Come"**. It may seem stupid to call your pooch when it is so close to you, but the whole point of this exercise is for them to learn that they should come to you when it hears the word "Come".

4. When your puppy comes to you, open your hand, and let them have their treat. Do not forget to praise verbally.

5. Step away from them again, and repeat the process until you are out of treats.

6. Make sure to increase the distance between you and your pup every day for even more effective training.

Tip: Most dog owners use the word "Come" when trying to bring their puppies inside. Coming in from outdoors is a disappointing and negative thing to puppies. By using this command to get your pooch inside, you may be poisoning the cue. Instead, try to use a different word for this action, such as "Inside".

Stand-Stay

"Stand" is a great command, but just like "Sit", it usually doesn't last for more than a couple of seconds. And while standing up is great for doing a quick paw wipe and avoiding getting mud all over your house, in some situations, you will need your pup to hold that position for a bit longer.

Fortunately, teaching your pooch to remain in a "Stand" position a bit longer is not that difficult. Just follow these next steps:

1. Kneel down in front of them.

2. Place your right hand on the puppy's collar, but make sure that your palm is out.

3. Slide your left hand under their belly.

4. Now, firmly say **"Stand-Stay"** as you gently prop your puppy into a standing position.

5. With your right hand relaxed, slide your left hand onto their thigh.

6. Wait for a couple of seconds and then release with **"Okay"**.

7. Increase the pause time gradually. You can start with 2-5 seconds, then try with 8, 12, 15, 20, until your pooch is ready to remain in that position for a full minute.

8. Repeat the previous steps. Once your pooch is standing still, let go. You may need to remind them to **"Stay"** halfway through.

9. Slide your hand from the collar, praise them verbally, and reward them with a yummy treat.

If practiced regularly, puppies don't need much time to catch on. However, if you are bumping into everyday resistance or your pooch is just too stubborn, they may need extra encouragement:

1. Depending on your puppy's height, place a handful of their favorite doggy treats where they can easily sniff them, but cannot reach them.
2. Instruct them to **"Stand-Stay"** in this position. `They will be encouraged to hold that position.
3. Give it a single treat and repeat **"Stand-Stay"** again.
4. Repeat this for as long as there are treats left.
5. After you give it the final treat, release with **"Okay"** and praise them immediately.
6. Increase the length between the treats, and decrease the number of treats, gradually. Ideally, you should be able to have one treat and have them remain that position for about a minute before giving them the reward. After you've managed that, you can start phasing out the reward and practice doing it without being lured.

6 to 9 Months

At this stage, your puppy is going through puberty. This is a pretty confusing time for your pooch, as the two conflicting forces guide their days: 1 – the desire to please you and 2 – the urge to walk his talk.

Communicating with a Pubescent Buddy

Establishing communication with your pubescent puppy is just like trying to talk some sense into your teenage kids – it may seem completely impossible. The most important thing here is to keep your cool, remain calm, and do not let yourself be the one behind the leash. Here are some tips on how to talk to your pooch during this stage:

- Detach – Although this one is not that much of a training technique, but more of a meditation practice that will help you keep your mental calmness, know that being centered can also positively affect your pup, too. Whenever you feel the pressure piling up, breathe in and out to detach yourself from your puppy. Don't take their behavior personally. Just remember that what you are doing will have tremendous results in the end. Be patient.

- Keep the Eye Contact – At this stage, your pooch is confused whether it is the follower or the leader. If you fail to get your puppy to look to you more than you look to him, you are definitely not the leader. If that's the case, reduce the attention you're giving your pooch. Pet them only when it is calm. And remember, always direct its behavior with eye contact.

- Don't Let Them Ignore You – Ignoring is a huge part of growing through puberty, and that is no different for dogs. It is your job, however, to avoid getting ignored by your puppy. If your puppy is on a leash and is challenging you on a direction, you should reinforce your expectation. If it simply ignores you when it is off the leash, withdraw from the situation immediately.

The Hand Signals

The treat is a great way to lure your puppy into cooperating and responding to your directions, as well as to reward the desired behavior. However, if you combine it with a hand signal, you will be able to improve your puppy's ability to focus, which will only contribute to a more successful training session.

Believe it or not, your puppy is able to begin learning hand signals once it is 3 or 4 months old, but I recommend putting an emphasis on this signal once your puppy has learned its directions. Why this period? Because now it is the time when you will most likely bump into resistance and you will need something to intensify your puppy's response.

You should use hand signals in front of their nose to make sure that the attention will be directed to you.

In most cases, the hand signal should be performed by pointing your finger and swinging your right arm from their nose to your face, in order to get your puppy's attention. Once you do that, you can instruct "Sit" or tell him "Okay" when it has been good.

You can also use different signals. For instance, you can flatten your palm in a paddle-like way, flash it in front of their nose and instruct "Stay".

Or you can point your finger and then sweep it from their nose to your eyes to encourage reconnection and get your pooch to "come" to you. If your puppy is far, however, you can get their attention by including a sweeping motion as you instruct them to "Come".

The TOP Directions

If you have been following the exercises from the previous stages regularly, chances are, your puppy already knows most of the commands. You should continue with regular training during this period as well, but now, you will need to extend your control on the directions that are the most familiar to them. Here are some directions that you should use most often:

Walking with "Heel"

You should continue using the "Heel" command to encourage proper walking, however, in this period, you should take your training to a more advanced level. Instead of teaching them in the comfort of your home, take "Heel" outside:

1. Attach the leash to their collar.
2. Let them walk ahead of you.
3. Now, instruct **"Heel"** firmly, and sap your left thigh with your hand.
4. Take a giant step backward gently, to lead your pup back to your side.
5. Once your pup is by your side, instruct the **"Sit"** command, before you release him with a positive **"Ok"**.
6. Make sure to praise immediately and reward with a giant treat for good behavior.

Reinforcing "Sit"

"Sit" is probably one of the first commands that your pup learns, but that doesn't mean that it shouldn't be practiced regularly once it learns how to heel or stand-stay. "Sit" is probably the politest direction, as most believe it to be the human equivalent to please. Make sure to ask your pooch to sit in all situations:

1. When there are distractions around (such as having a new guest over), instruct your pup to **"Sit".**

2. It will probably just ignore you. (If it doesn't, praise them immediately, and try to practice "Sit" in even more distracting situations).

3. If it ignores you, say **"No"**, and do not give them any attention for some time.

4. Now, try it again, only this time, lure them with a treat. It will probably sit down. Praise and give them the treat.

5. Wait a few minutes before instructing **"Sit"** again, without the treat. If it still doesn't respond, say **"No"** again, place the treat beside you, and do not let them have it.

6. This probably seems easier than it is, but don't lose patience. Practice this exercise for as long as it takes for your pup to learn how to sit on command even with distractions around.

Using "Down" Frequently

"Down" is a direction that can be of great use. Continue to use it often, even in those situations when your puppy doesn't want to cooperate. If that's the case, simply position your pup by gently pressing the pressure point that is between its shoulder blades, while lifting one of its paws to shift the balance. If it starts rolling on the floor or tries to nip your toes, ignore them completely. Many dog trainers say that it helps if you step on the leash when dealing with a naughty dog. That way the dog is only allowed to lie down comfortably, so you can give this a try when faced with one of their tantrums. Release only after they has calmed down.

Try to use "Down" in all kinds of situations. For instance, use it before treating. Instruct them to get down before allowing them to take the treat. Or, use it before dinner. Cover their food bowl with your hand, and instruct them "Down" as you're putting the bowl down.

Taking "No" Outside

Once your puppy learns what "No" means, it is time to take it outside and test if they will still be cooperative even when the wonders of the outdoor world are involved. Practice "No" when the neighbor's cat is around, when there are kids in the park, where your puppy gets distracted by bikers, and is amused by other passing-by temptations.

But, do not try to teach "No" outside when your puppy is unleashed. You may end up chasing them all around the park. Train them to accept "No" when their leash is attached to their collar, and always correct with a sharp and sternest tone.

"Wait" with Distractions

Just like "Sit", this is the period when you have to practice "Wait", but with a lot of distractions involved. Use the same method as with "Sit", try to ignore them if it is being naughty, lure with a treat, try without the treat again, and finally, punish by not allowing them to have the treat, by refusing to give outdoor access, etc. You'd be surprised to learn how well negative reinforcement actually works.

9 to 12 Months

Now that your pup is a teenager, they will begin testing your boundaries, not only to see if it can be cut some slack, but also because it is emotionally more ready and gets more confused by some of your directions. It wonders, perhaps whether instructing the "Down" command when there is only the two of you in the room is different than directing it to lay "Down" when there is company around.

Keep in mind that it is perfectly normal for your pup to be questioning you in this period. If you have been training them from the start and you know that it has managed to learn most of the commands but suddenly shows resistance or takes a bit too long to perform a familiar action, that means that it is questioning your directions.

There is really no other way to get through this period except with patience and persistence. Just remember the two most important things:

1. Decide exactly what you want your pup to do when giving them a direction

2. Always follow through. If your expectations are not crystal clear, how can you expect for your puppy's reaction to be?

If you keep bumping into resistance a bit too often, start using the "No" command more. Alternatively, try the ignoring technique:

1. If your pup is questioning you by not responding to your direction the way they should, stop immediately.

2. If you are at home, go to another room. Do not let your pup see you for a couple of minutes. If you are outside. Stand still and do not move. Take out your phone to check your messages or just look the other way for a minute or two. The point is for you to stop all interactions with them.

3. After ignoring them for a couple of minutes, repeat the given direction again.

4. If it still is not behaving the way it should, ignore them a little bit longer this time. The point is for your puppy to learn that undesired behavior has an undesired outcome, which in this case is you not giving them any attention.

Giving the Clicker a Try

Positive reinforcement is, perhaps, the greatest way for puppies to learn which actions please you and treat them. With the power of the reward, your pup gets encouraged to repeat these actions again in the future, until eventually, they become their normal behavior. But sometimes, even when your pockets are filled with the yummiest doggy treats, the positive training process may progress at a much slower pace than expected. If this happens, do not give up on your pup just yet. There is a trick for you to speed things up a bit and teach them obedience. That trick is called *clicker training*.

Clicker training is a training technique that is combined with or used instead of the normal positive reinforcement routine in order to teach puppies to repeat the behavior that rewards them and avoid those actions that offer no benefit to them. Here, the pup learns that it is the one that controls the outcome, feels more in charge of the training, and is less likely to get overwhelmed by the whole process. Besides being super empowering, clicker training also helps pups look forward to the training sessions, and improve your ability to communicate with your dog.

How Does It Work?

Unlike a normal positive reinforcement training -where you teach your pup a command word - here, you let your pup accidentally stumble upon the desired behavior. For instance, it may perform many "wrong" actions during the day, until it accidentally sits down. Once you see that happening, you give the clicker *a click* and instantly reward your pup. The ultimate goal here is for your pup to associate its action with the click, which it will then associate with the reward, and will get encouraged to repeat that behavior again. To them, the sound of the click equals great things happening.

With clicker training, you use neither commands, physical directions, or any kind of punishment. Here, the process is entirely puppy motivated, and the pup is given the choice to discover what's right and what's wrong, on their own.

Click Equals Treat

In order for you to be able to let your pup learn that a certain behavior is desired, you first need to help them figure out that the sound of the clicker gives them the rewards. Here is how you can make that happen:

1. Fill a shallow dish with some of your pup's favorite doggy treats. Let them sniff you and acknowledge that it is there, but don't let them have any just yet.

2. Sit down on the floor, have the treat dish within your reach, and get comfortable. Grab a treat with one hand and hold the clicker with the other one.

3. Now, *click* the clicker and wait for your pup to come to explore. Chances are, as soon as it hears the sound, their ear antennas will twitch and they will come to investigate where the sound came from.

4. As soon as it comes to you and you see that the *click* has managed to pique its interest, give them a treat. They will probably be confused, not knowing why it is rewarded, but it will also probably not care at first. Just let them enjoy their treat.

5. Repeat this process again. Just remember to always click first, and then treat. Your puppy must learn that the sound of the clicker means that it is getting rewarded.

6. When your pup's attention moves from the clicker to your hand, as soon as it hears the *click,* that means that it has already figured out that click equals treat.

7. Once they know what the click signal means, you can use this to point out those actions that you want your pup to repeat. You simply wait for the puppy to perform the desired action first. Once it, puts down its tail to sit, for instance, you immediately click and give them the treat right after it has acknowledged the sound.

8. They may be confused at first, but they will want to understand what made the click sound. And that is the whole point of the clicker training; to allow the puppy to figure things out on their own.

9. Since puppies understand cause-and-effect very well, they will most likely start performing all sorts of different actions in an attempt to hear the click and get the

reward. This gives you the opportunity to make a selection of which behavior you want to encourage and also teach your pup which actions it is not getting rewarded for.

Should You Use It?

The clicker is a great way for pups to learn on their own, sure. And it will definitely help them determine which behavior is desired and what actions aren't, there is no doubt about that. However, if you are thinking about replacing the regular positive reinforcement training with the clicker training, you will be making a huge mistake. Why?

The clicker works great if you want to teach your pup a few tricks and show off with your training skills in front of your friends and family. However, when trying to teach obedience, you are in for some disappointment. Since the clicker training doesn't come with command words or other directions that may show the pup the right way, your puppy will never know when the right action is desired.

For instance, if you want your puppy to settle down when you have some guests over and you give the clicker a click, they will not know what is expected of them. Is it to sit down? Play dead? Lift up his paw?

That's why the clicker is not the best option when it comes to teaching discipline. However, you can use the clicker in a combination with your regular positive reinforcement training in order to further encourage your pup to behave better:

1. Simply. choose a command word and follow the steps as instructed in the previous chapter.
2. Before you praise and reward your pup, give the clicker a click. When they acknowledge the sound, say "Good Boy/Girl" and treat as usual.
3. The clicker will help the pup associate the good behavior with the reward and may speed up the training process.

To wrap it up, no, you shouldn't use the clicker as the only obedience training technique, as not receiving clear direction for instilling order can only confuse your bundle of joy. However, if you are dealing with a stubborn pup or your training simply doesn't progress as desired, you can definitely try incorporating the clicker into your regular routine to motivate your puppy to be more cooperative.

Correcting Behavior Problems

You have a puppy. Let's face it, there will be a lot of naughtiness around your house, and that is all normal. Puppies have a lot to learn on their way to becoming adult dogs, and that includes testing your limits and pushing the boundaries to see how far you will actually let them go.

Bad behavior is part of the deal of adopting a puppy. You should be aware that it is in your puppy's nature to show over excitement in ways you find unacceptable. Just like it is a natural thing to be stressed. It is your job to pin-point the reason for the bad behavior, eradicate the culprit, and completely redirect your puppy with nothing but love and understanding.

Correcting behavioral problems requires time and patience, but approaching the issue with an exaggerated reaction can set both you and your puppy to a path that is much harder to come back from.

Shushing the Barker

Having a constant barker in your home is no fun. Being robbed from your good night's sleep is nothing but a headache. But before you try to find a way to shush your barking ball of fur, you first need to determine what makes your pooch bark in the first place. Barking is a dog's way of communicating, and it is how they express themselves. See what your pooch is trying to tell you before you take a step further:

Barking for Attention

Your puppy just has to go through a phase of not being able to bear being alone. It is a normal part of their development. If your puppy is a loud barker when you are preparing to leave the house, here are some tips that may help you solve the problem:

- Do not give them attention. By soothing a protester, you only add fuel to the fire. You will not only make things worse, but you will end up with a spoiled pup.

- Do not leave or enter your house in a grandiose way because they are too exciting for your pup and they're only encouraging the barking even more.

- Grab a hollow bone that is safe for your pup to chew on and fill it with some peanut butter. Offer it to your pup before you leave the house to keep them occupied.

You can also try this:

1. Grab an empty can and put it in your pocket.

2. Get ready to leave the house and stand in the hallway.

3. Chances are, your puppy is already barking their lungs out. Throw the can toward (NOT AT your puppy). The goal here is for them to think that this reaction comes from the environment, not you.

4. When your puppy stops barking, give them attention.

5. Do this for every arrival and departure, until it realizes that stopping means getting the attention.

Barking at Everything

If your puppy is a real barker, then chances are, nothing in your home goes unnoticed. But, living with everlasting barking can be a real pain. If nothing is wrong with them, and you know that it is just an incessant barker, then know that the reason it is doing that is probably because it wants things to go away. For instance, if it barks at a cat, the cat will most likely go away. But if it starts barking at the postman, it may realize that their superpowers aren't as effective. So it will start barking some more and more. And then louder and louder.

If your first thought is to try yelling at them to stop (which is quite understandable given that his barking has become the soundtrack of your life), you will only make things worse. To dogs, yelling is the human way of barking. If you start yelling, they will only think that you are barking too, and that will lead to – that's right – more barking.

There are three things you can do to try to solve this issue:

1. Start (or intensify) training. Your pooch most likely thinks it is the leader and gets ego boosts as he is probably thinking that is his duty to guard the territory. By starting or devoting to a more intense training routine, you will let them know that it is actually you who is in charge of the home and that there are some rules to be followed.

2. Block off lookout posts. If your pup spends a lot of time in front of the window, guarding and keeping eye on things, make sure to block his access. If necessary, crate them more

or secure them with a lead that is long enough for them just to lie down comfortably. Increase freedom gradually as your pooch becomes less interested in barking.

3. Avoid leaving them alone outdoors. If your pooch is confined and unsupervised for longer periods of time, that will only lead to territorial behavior and allow for boredom to swoop in, both of which are usually followed with long and loud periods of barking.

If neither of these seem to do the trick, maybe you can start teaching him new words. Teaching him *Speak* and *Quit* may help you put a stop to their excessive barking:

1. First, you need to teach your pup that *Speak* means *start barking*. To begin this, simulate a visitor. Knock on the door or ring the bell. Make sure that your pocket is filled with doggy treats.

2. The second your pup starts barking say **"Speak"** in a firm tone.

3. Praise and reward them immediately.

4. Do this for a couple of days, until your puppy learns what *speak* means.

5. Once your pup starts barking when you give them the *speak* command, it is time to teach them to be quiet. Instruct your pup to **"Speak"**.

6. Once it starts barking, say **"Quiet"** in a firm tone.

7. Wait for your pup to stop barking. If needed, say **"Quiet"** again.

8. It may take a while for your pup to stop barking, and that's okay. The second it stops, praise them like crazy and give it a treat.

9. Respond for as long as it takes for your pooch to learn that *quiet* means *stop barking*.

Once your pup learns that, you can use this command to shush them whenever their barking starts getting just a bit too much.

Not Accepting Biting

In the first couple of weeks, biting is a normal daily hassle. But while soft mouthing is okay when your pup is playing with you, for some people, it can be a scary, if not a traumatic experience. It is extremely important for you to teach your puppy that their razor-sharp teeth are not made for the human skin while it is still a young pup in order for them to learn right from the start what it cannot play bite with. Not to mention that this may prevent future injuries and even save you from a big fat lawsuit.

This training technique will discourage your pup to bite your skin as a part of its games:

1. Place one of your hands in your pup's mouth and shake it gently until it realizes that you want to play with them.

2. Play with your pup for a while. As long as it is soft-mouthing you and doesn't apply pressure, let them have his fun. The second you feel their teeth piercing a bit sharper, say **"Ouch"** or another negative word, take your hand out, and stop playing with them.

3. Step aside, look away, and do not interact with them for about 30 seconds. Do this for about 5-6 times a day.

4. If your pup doesn't let go of your hand the second you say "Ouch", leave the room immediately and do not let your pup see you for a couple of minutes.

5. When your pup finally realizes that *ouch* means that *it is time to let go of the hand*, you can start teaching them that they shouldn't play biting with humans under no circumstances.

6. It may take a while for you to get your pup to realize that it shouldn't play biting at all, but you should be patient. To start, simply play with your dog and keep your hand close to its mouth, however, do not place it inside.

7. Wait until your pup starts biting. The second it touches your skin with its teeth, even if it is super gently, say **"Bad Boy/Girl"** or another similar word, get up, and stop interacting with them for a couple of minutes.

8. Do this every time their teeth meet your skin. This way they will eventually learn that biting is unacceptable.

Getting Chewing Under Control

You cannot exactly train your pup not to chew on things, and you should not even try. Chewing is not only a natural instinct and an interesting way to spend their time, but it also contributes to their physical and mental health. By chewing, your pup supports the flow of antibacterial saliva and keeps his gums and teeth stay healthy and strong. That is why appropriate chew toys can jumpstart the healthy development of puppy's permanent teeth and make the whole process a lot less painful.

However, just because it is supposed to chew on things doesn't mean that your new sofa should be all chewed-up. Besides providing rubber toys, appropriate ropes, and marrow bones, there are also some other tricks that can help your pooch keep his teeth away from your possessions:

- Allow plenty of exercise. Most dogs start a chewing contest when they are bored or when they have a fair amount of extra energy that they have to channel somewhere. If you don't want your couch to be that place, make sure to take your puppy on longer walks in order to knock down their urge to chew on things inside the house.

- Use taste deterrents. Taste deterrents are nasty-tasting liquids sold in spray bottles that you can use to discourage the pup from chewing on things. You can find them in most pet stores, and they are pretty cost-effective as your pup will not like the idea of chewing on something that tastes awful. These deterrents usually have no scent at all, so you shouldn't worry about having an unpleasant smell spreading inside your house. Bitter apple is a great choice for a taste deterrent.

  When you notice them chewing on something inappropriate, simply grab the spray bottle and spray that object immediately, and let them notice you. After doing so, offer them a safe toy that they can chew on to encourage appropriate behavior.

- Play a "No" and "Good Boy/Girl" game. Lay out several objects on the floor, among which you will place a couple of chew toys. Wait for them to grab an object. If it is an appropriate chewable, say "Good Boy/Girl". If not, say "No" to let your puppy know it should let go of the object.

- Praise them. In many cases, puppies are encouraged to chew on their toys when they are encouraged to do so. Whenever you see them chewing on their toys, praise them to mark the good behavior, and then give them a treat as a reward.

Stopping the Digging Frenzy

If those muddy paws freak you out, relax. You need to learn to accept this behavior as a part of the normal canine instinct. But just because it is natural, it doesn't mean that it is okay for your pup to be passing their time turning your backyard into a construction site. Whether your puppy is fussy, stressed, or just bored, you will need to find a way to make them learn that digging whenever and wherever he feels like it is not acceptable.

Although just like chewing, you cannot exactly train them not to dig. However, there are a few tricks you can do that will discourage this action. The very first thing is to offer a digging spot for your puppy:

1. Pick an area in your backyard that your puppy can use for digging. Make sure to mark the territory so it's easy to distinguish where it's ok to dig and where it's not. If you leave in an apartment, you can provide a sandbox for digging in your bathroom from time to time, or you can even do this with a certain spot in the nearest park.

2. Bring toys to that spot, or even better, bury treats there to encourage your pup to be digging there.

3. Take your pup to that spot on a daily basis and encourage them to dig by instructing her **"Go Dig"** or another command by your choice.

4. When you catch your puppy in the act of digging someplace else, correct with a firm **"No"**.

You can also give some other tricks a try:

- Dogs really dislike the citrus scent. Putting lemon or orange peels in the holes will most likely discourage your pooch from digging there.

- To help your pup learn that digging in certain areas in your yard is not acceptable, you can install some sensors such as sprinkles there.

- Do not spray your pooch with a hose when you catch them in the act. This is a common correction method that many dog owners use, however, this is not only cruel, but it will also make him dig even more if it gets all fussy. Instead, you can try burying some of its own feces. Dogs usually hate the smell and taste of their own feces, so give this a try if nothing else helps.

- Many dogs dig excessively when they are left alone. If that is the case, see if you can leave your pup indoors when leaving the house for a couple of hours.

Discouraging the Jumper

Dogs are social animals. It is in their nature to seek and give attention, as well as to show excitement and lavish us with love when we enter the door. Isn't that one of the main reasons why most people adopt puppies in the first place? Having a small pup jumping up every time he lays eyes on you is cute, but if this behavior is left unchecked, this can easily turn into a 60-pound force trying to knock you over. And that is something that you will begin dreading.

Jumping up is one of those behaviors that dog owners love to hate. Why? Because they usually start as a cute thing that the pup gets rewards for, and then quickly turn into something that can cause an injury to both the dog and the owner. So, what am I trying to say here? Never encourage a pup who is jumping up by rewarding the behavior. And I am not only talking about a reward in the form of a tasty treat. When a pup is jumping up, the reward it is seeking for is your attention. Rob it from that and they will soon stop performing the action that does not elicit the favorable outcome.

Turning Away from the Jump

When your pup jumps, the best response is to simply turn away from it. It may be heartbreaking not to give your pup attention when it is so excited to see you, but this is the most effective way to teach him to control their emotions, and believe me, once it grows into an adult dog, this trick you're teaching them now will be greatly appreciated.

Bring your hands to your chest and avoid eye contact. Once your pup sees that it gets no response, it will soon settle down. Once it is four-on-the-floor, praise them for being calm and reward them with your attention now.

Use Commands

If your pup has already mastered the "Sit" command, you can use this to get it to settle down. Again, as soon as it is on the floor, praise and reward immediately.

Go Out the Door

When you enter your door and you see your pup all excited and jumping up, simply open the door, step aside, and then close the door. Wait for your pup to calm down before going back inside. If your pooch starts jumping up again, repeat this process. Now, this may take a while, but don't lose faith. Your pup will soon pick up that you will not go through unless it greets you in a calm way. Once it does that, praise them like crazy and reward them with your attention. Or a smelly treat. No dog has ever refused that.

Dealing with Separation Anxiety

Puppies hate being left alone. If it is up to them, they will probably follow you to the end of the World. But, they cannot. As much as you both enjoy your time together, there are times when you simply have to leave your pooch alone, and chances are, you have to do it on a daily basis. But just because you hear sad whining when you close the door doesn't mean that your pup is anxious you left them alone. In order for you to be able to help them cope better with separation, you will first need to determine whether it really is anxious or not.

So, what are the signs of separation anxiety in puppies? If your pup is chewing things destructively when left alone, keeps urinating and defecating even if it is house trained, is barking, howling, and whining excessively, develops a habit of excessive digging or keeps scratching the door as an attempt to reunite with you, chances are, your pooch is suffering from separation anxiety.

Do not despair! This is completely normal and it happens in the majority of cases when the dog owner has a full-time job that requires them to leave the house for longer periods of time.

Here are some tips that can help you knock down the anxiety and boost the mood of your pooch a bit while you are away:

- Do not make departures and arrivals a big deal. Keep ignoring your pup while getting ready to leave the house, and then gently pet them on the head before you leave the door. Do not turn to mush with them only to show them your back and close the door. Leaving with kisses and treats will not reassure your pooch. Quite the contrary. That will only leave them stressed out.

- Come up with a "Goodbye" word that you will use every time you leave your home. That will reassure your pup that you will actually get back.

- Make sure to leave the area where the pup will be staying dimly lit, so you can encourage sleep.

- Always leave toys around. Giving your pup something to chew on while alone is a great way for them to keep boredom at bay and not think about being left alone that much.

- If needed, leave the radio on playing relaxing music such as classical music or jazz, if you need to cover unfamiliar sounds and offer reassurance. The best advice is to play that music even when you are together in the house so that your pup will get used to it.

- Spend some time near their crate so that their safe haven will smell like you even after you leave the house. Some owners even leave recently worn pieces of clothes around so that the area will still have a strong scent of you.

- If you come home only to find a mess, do not yell or correct your pup. The correction will not be associated with the destruction that the puppy has caused, but with your arrival. Instead of teaching them to be more disciplined in the future, you are actually contributing to them feeling even more anxious the next time you leave the house. Instead of correcting, try to find a different approach to ensure that the destructive behavior will not happen again.

- If your pup is suffering from severe separation anxiety, consult with your veterinarian. They may suggest you hire a dog walker to take them on long walks, or even for you to sign your puppy up for a doggie daycare.

Keep in mind that separation anxiety is not a result of lack of training. This form of anxiety and obedience have nothing in common, so don't fool yourself into thinking that insufficient training is what causes your pooch to behave destructively when you leave the door. Follow the tips above and see if you can offer reassurance. If you keep providing reassurance from the early stages, your pup will soon learn to accept the routine and you will have no problem to leave your full-grown dog alone when going out in the future. Give it some time and be patient.

Conclusion

Puppies thrive on strictly set routines. If you manage to make the training process a fun and consistent process, your pooch will be encouraged to learn the desired directions in a short period of time.

With the help of this book, you will be able to master all the true-and-tried puppy training techniques and help your puppy grow into an obedient and happy dog that will act respectfully.

Just remember that you are the one leading the way. It is in your puppy's nature to follow, so make sure to show them the right way. The secret formula to obedient puppyhood = patience + persistence. Equip yourself with these qualities and see how strong your owner-dog relationship can really be.

Positive Dog Training 101

The Practical Guide to Training Your Dog the Loving and Friendly Way Without Causing Your Dog Stress or Harm Using Positive Reinforcement

Table of Contents

Introduction 94

Training With Love 95
- THE POWER OF REINFORCEMENT 95
- THE SCIENCE BEHIND POSITIVE REINFORCEMENT 100

Reinforcing Proper Behavior 102

House Training An Older Dog 104
- GETTING READY 104
- CRATE TRAINING (IN 1 WEEKEND) 105
- GOING POTTY 109
- PAPER TRAINING 111

Teaching Behavior In 4 Weeks 114
- WHERE TO TRAIN BUDDY? 114
- THE BASIC FORMULA 115
- WEEK 1 TRAINING 116
- WEEK 2 TRAINING 124
- WEEK 3 TRAINING 131
- WEEK 4 TRAINING 140

Dealing With Misbehavior 148
- EXCESSIVE BARKING 148
- DISCOURAGING JUMPING UP 150
- NO BEGGING, PLEASE 153
- STOP LICKING ME... OR YOURSELF 154
- STOPPING SUBMISSIVE WETTING 156

Fun Games For Practice And Bonding 159
- HIGH-FIVE 159
- ROLL OVER 161
- TUG 162
- PLAY DEAD 163

- Belly Crawl 164
- Take A Bow 165

Phasing Out The Treats 167
- The Food Lures 167
- The Food Rewards 168

Addressing Anxiety Correctly 170

Bonus Chapter: Agility Training 174

Conclusion 177

Introduction

Whether you have just adopted an older dog and are looking for a way to set some boundaries or it was your lack of commitment that made you skip the puppy training phase – do not worry – training an adult dog who already has established a certain way of doing things is indeed possible.

Step away from the traditional way of training and enter the rewarding world of positive reinforcement. Give your dog a reason to behave, and he will! Filled with positive and loving training techniques that will not only teach behavior in just 4 weeks but also form a strong and lasting dog-owner bond, this book will help you prepare your furry friend for his canine citizenship and enjoy hassle-free long walks in the park, filled with fun games, joy, and love.

It doesn't matter if you are dealing with a stubborn, fearful, or an already-trained dog. This guide can not only help you start the training from scratch, but it will also give you amazing ideas on how to continue practicing good behavior and instilling discipline so that your dog will maintain his good manners.

From a four weeks' worth of training plan and the best house training techniques, to the best ways to put a stop to misbehavior problems, teach fun and enjoyable games, as well as keep Buddy fit with agility training, turning your adult Buddy into the most well-behaved ball of fur requires nothing more than the content in this book. And the yummy freeze-dried liver, of course.

Training with Love

They say that dogs are man's best friend. That there is a true and meaningful emotional connection between the canine and its human owner. But even though experts confirm that the human-dog bond is positive and everlasting, it is pretty impossible to believe that you are Buddy's most important thing in the world when your huge ball of fur makes chewed-up shoes, torn-up belongings, and being-woken-up-by-excessive-barking just a part of your day-to-day living. Can you really bring order back to your house?

Mention that you have a disobedient dog to trainers that have been doing their jobs for 20+ years, and you will most likely get the same answer – the choke-chain training method is the only way to go. But is physically forcing your dog to listen to you really the right way to form a loving dog-owner relationship? Do you force your partner to love you as well? No, you lay out the foundation of a strong relationship with love and understanding. So why should training your dog be any different?

If you think that the positive dog training method is just one of those fads and crazes that modern society has come up with, you couldn't be more wrong. Teaching your dog good behavior while showing him love and respect has proven to be the most effective. If having a partner for life was the reason you adopted Buddy in the first place, then reinforcing his behavior in a positive way is definitely what you should do in order to instill discipline.

The Power of Reinforcement

If you are considering training your dog in a positive way, then you have to understand what the most important training tool – *the reinforcement* – really means.

Although the term 'reinforcement' is often mistakenly used by traditional trainers as a way of punishing your dog, the truth is, reinforcing your pet represents the contrary of punishment. So, if punishing your dog would mean decreasing the dog's behavior, reinforcing him would mean the opposite, or increasing the desired behaviors.

To put it simply, if you purposefully reinforce the actions your dog does, he will be encouraged to do them more often, which is why reinforcement is such a huge help in the dog training process.

How Does it Work?

It all sounds very simple, but how does reinforcement really work? It works by assigning consequences to different actions. Because that's how every living creature learns, really. Through the consequences of their behavior.

That also applies to your dog. Your Buddy is able to store a memory of the outcomes of his actions, and allocate that memory as *good, bad,* or in some cases, *indifferent*. When he thinks a certain action will provide him a good consequence, he is encouraged to perform that action in order to reap the benefits. Similarly, when he finds that some behavior will most likely result in a bad (or indifferent) result, his brain will automatically discourage him from performing that action.

To train your dog to be disciplined and polite, you will have to help him associate good behavior with good consequences in order for him to be encouraged to perform them again in the future. It sounds very simple, I know, but in reality, it is somewhat trickier than that.

Reinforcement is the most helpful training tool, that is true, but it is also a double-edged sword. Why? Because reinforcement isn't only created by you. It can also be discovered by accident.

For instance, if there is always food available on your kitchen island that Buddy can steal, he will learn that jumping up onto tables is a behavior that is rewarding and, therefore, should be repeated. Now, you may think this is simply an act of disobedience, but here, the truth is that Buddy was simply encouraged to learn this behavior. Your dog cannot really differentiate the behaviors he learns by accident from those that you train him to understand. His brain works in a simple way – repeat what is beneficial to you.

With positive training, you can encourage the desired actions, as well as discourage the ones that are not.

Positive vs Negative Reinforcement

When it comes to training with reinforcement, there are two distinctive types here: positive and negative. But although the first thing that comes to mind when mentioning positive and negative is good and bad, the truth is, positive and negative reinforcement do not represent the nice and the nasty. Their origin can be found in mathematics.

Positive and negative reinforcement means *adding* and *taking away* something. They are not good and bad, and they surely cannot be classified as rewarding and punishing. Why? Because there are no punishments in training with reinforcement. So what do they mean?

Positive Reinforcement– Positive reinforcement means adding something in order to increase (or reinforce) the dog's desired behavior. The most popular – and most convenient – way of reinforcing the dog's actions is by giving him rewards. For instance, giving Buddy a biscuit for taking a seat.

That's called positive reinforcement because the dog finds the added reward pleasant. The goal here is for the dog to associate the behavior with the reward, so he can be encouraged to repeat the same action again in the future, with the purpose of getting the tasty treat again, of course.

But even though the food rewards are the most common, you can also reinforce the dog's behavior by giving him attention, playing a fun game with him, granting access to someplace he enjoys being at, etc.

Negative Reinforcement – Negative reinforcement, on the other hand, means the opposite of adding. It means subtracting something, but even though most mistakenly confuse this term with taking away some things that the dog finds pleasant in order to punish or correct, negative reinforcement actually takes away the things that the dog finds unpleasant.

For instance, the trainer applies pressure to get the dog into a sitting position and then takes away the physical discomfort by releasing the force, when the dog is already sitting down and, therefore, carries out the desired action.

Negative and positive reinforcements do not go hand in hand, and you will not find a dog trainer that uses them both. We are discussing the negative reinforcement now in order to understand that this term does not represent correcting or punishing your dog, as can be found on many dog websites and blogs.

So, How Do You Correct a Behavior?

Where there is reinforcement, there are no punishments. However, despite the fact that you will be training your dog with the most positive and pleasant methods, there will be times when you will simply have to intervene.

For instance, if your pup refuses to come to you when out in the park, and he decides that playing with his ball is way more fun than walking at heel, you will obviously need to do something in order to let him know that his behavior is unacceptable. Here, the best tactic is to simply take away his ball. This is punishment, yes. But the time when the punishment occurs is of great significance.

If you feel that there is a strong need for you to take a toy away from your dog at the beginning of the training, then, by all means, do it. But know that positive reinforcement and punishments do not go hand in hand because once the dog is trained, there is no need to correct his behavior. A trained dog is supposed to come to you when called, not refuse to cooperate. You may find it necessary to yell "No" or take his toy away from him at the beginning of the training, while your dog is still disobedient.

Once you train your dog with positive reinforcement, he will be able to perform the desired actions with ease. The only way to correct a behavior is with training. You can train Buddy to let go of his misbehavior with positive reinforcement as well, which we will discuss in more detail later in this book.

To sum up, you can sometimes decide on a humane punishment such as taking a toy away or not allowing access to an area, but only while still in the process of training. Just keep in mind that by taking his toy away, you are not teaching Buddy a lesson. You cannot create new behaviors with punishments. It's impossible, and it will only contribute to decreased cooperation out of the fear of receiving punishment. Once your dog masters the basic commands and is ready to learn new behaviors, you should avoid empty punishments, but strive to teach good behavior so that Buddy can learn how to properly behave, permanently. By incorporating positive reinforcement techniques, you help your dog understand what is asked of him and repeat the good behavior in the long term.

It's All in the Timing

If you poke a bear with a stick, the animal will get angry and ready to attack right there and right then. The bear will not leave for a few minutes to think about it and then come back later to finish its job. Your action will have immediate consequences.

We've all evolved to learn that way, and so has your dog. You can only teach him decent behavior if you reward the desired action immediately after it has happened. It's no use treating your dog for sitting down a few minutes after he puts his bottom on the floor. Buddy can associate the reward with the action only if he is given the treat immediately after performing it.

So, if you want to train your dog the right way, you need to understand that it's all in the timing. Praise and reward should be given to Buddy the second he has completed the desired actions. Otherwise, he will never be able to truly understand why he is getting all the rewards, and you will never be able to train him properly.

The Benefits

The best thing about positive reinforcement is that it allows you to teach your dog good behavior in a positive and humane way while keeping his confidence up at the same time. Dog owners who use this training method report fewer behavioral problems than those who choose more traditional training techniques. Getting your dog to behave on a day-to-day basis is most effective if the dog sees something in it for him as well.

But besides it being super effective, positive reinforcement comes with a set of other benefits as well. Some of them are:

- Positive reinforcement trains Buddy toward good behavior, rather than only toward responses.

- The training is an enjoyable and fun experience for both you and your dog, and unlike the traditional methods, it feels less of a task.

- It helps you build a healthy and strong bond between you and Buddy.

- It will improve your communication with your dog.

- Every member of your family can be involved in the training process; you are not the only person in charge.

- It can be a great exercise for your dog, allowing Buddy to burn off tons of energy.

- It can be used for many behavioral issues. For instance, if you have an aggressive dog, punishing him traditionally may make the situation worse. Positive reinforcement can help you find the perfect way to correct misbehavior and instill proper habits.

The Science Behind Positive Reinforcement

Over the last couple of decades, there has been a serious shift towards less punitive dog training techniques. Today, the words 'dominance,' 'respect,' and 'pack leader' have very little meaning in the process of training. If you observe a modern trainer teaching dogs simple commands, you will see how different and more humane they are than those old school dog lessons that our parents (and some of us – no need to beat yourself up over it) were used to in the past.

But even though there are more and more positive dog trainers, there are still those who look at positive reinforcement as nothing but a way of creating spoiled dogs. If you, too, are wondering whether all those rewards, treats, and smooches will only contribute to Buddy becoming addicted to them and will eventually turn to naughtiness only to get them, you cannot be more wrong.

Positive and permissive are two very different things. You are training with positivity, and although it may look like you are pleading with your dog and begging him to perform a simple task, that's far from the truth. Positive reinforcement may depend on luring your dog into participating in the process, but that's only short-term. The reward is a great encouragement tool that will help your dog to be more involved and learn sooner. Once he adopts proper habits, the rewards will be phased out.

Those who best understand this are, perhaps, those people who have already made the shift from traditional to positive and have experienced both worlds first-hand. If you are not one of those people or don't know anyone who can vouch for the efficiency of this method, then perhaps the multiple studies and scientific results will be convincing enough for you to give positive reinforcement a try.

Dominance is Outdated

A study published by the Clinical Veterinary Sciences under the University of Bristol has found that the aggression in dogs has nothing to do with them trying to assert dominance over their owners.

By spending over 6 months studying freely-interacting dogs, the researchers found that dogs are not motivated to keep their place in the pack's order, as many trainers think. In fact, these academics say that 'dominance decreasing' techniques are not only worthless, but they can also be dangerous and worsen the canine's behavior.

Punishment Leads to Disobedience

In the "Applied Animal Behaviour Science" journal from 2010, there is published a study that shows the correlation between the dog's behavior, the inconsistent level of the owner's engagement in activities, and regular punishments. The analysis of 1276 Quaternary helped the researchers conclude that regular use of punishments only increases excitability and anxiety in dogs while using rewards can calm and distract the canine.

This study also concluded that not engaging in regular activities with the dog can also lead to behavioral problems. It's easy to understand that reward-based training can decrease the misbehavior and knock down fear-related anxiety and aggression.

Positive Reinforcements Instead of Positive Punishments and Negative Reinforcements

A study from 217, published in the "Journal of Veterinary Behavior," has concluded that aversive training methods such as training with negative reinforcements or using positive punishments can have a significant negative impact on the dog's physical and mental health.

The study has found that even though positive punishments can be effective to some extent, they are not more beneficial than the positive reinforcements training method. In fact, the evidence showed that it is quite the opposite. Dog owners should train their dogs with positive reinforcements instead of positive punishments or negative reinforcements, in order to instill disobedience and maintain the welfare state of their dog.

Reinforcing Proper Behavior

Think of training as a two-way street. It is not just you who has to give 100 percent; your dog is just as involved in the process as you are. It doesn't seem so in the beginning, because you don't start off as the trainer, but the student. Yes, you've read it correctly. You are the S T U D E N T. How? Because Buddy is already used to training you. Most of you probably think that I am talking nonsense, but if you give it some thought, you will see that I am, in fact, right.

Dogs know what is to their advantage and what's not – it is a skill that they have used since the day they were born. And they don't think twice about getting what they want. In fact, everything they do is about getting what they want. Take begging at the table, for example. Buddy will beg and whine, and touch you with his nose and paws, until you give up and give him a slice of meat. Or think about this scenario. You are sitting on the couch watching TV when Buddy decides to drop a ball in your lap. You instantly pick up the ball and throw it to your dog. See? He has indeed trained you well. And there is nothing wrong with that, either. You just have to think about which actions you really want to reinforce. Because after all, the whole point of training is about reinforcing good behavior.

Speaking of reinforcement, here is where your attitude plays a huge part. How you approach the training is of great importance. During training, you need to maintain a positive attitude in order to reinforce the proper behavior and not mistakenly create an aversion towards something. For instance, let's say that you are running late for work and you have to put Buddy in his crate. You call and call for him, but he is nowhere to be found. All of a sudden, he walks into the house through the back door with muddy paws. He has been digging. You are now furious that you will have to be even more late thanks to the fact that you have some wiping and sweeping to do. So, what's your first impression? You give him a good scolding. And, what will be Buddy's thoughts? *He called me, I came, he got angry.* Your dog may have a guilty look on his face, but that is surely not because he understands that he has made a mess. Dogs look guilty because you get angry. And, in this case, by getting angry, you are only contributing to Buddy associating *"Come boy"* with *getting angry and yelling.* Do you think he will come to you next time you call him?

You have to be very careful about your attitude and reactions because they are what creates Buddy's responses. If you want to reinforce the proper behavior, you need to address it directly.

If you ask your dog to come, you cannot start yelling about the fact that he made a mess. Instead, you praise him for coming to you. If you catch him in the act of digging, only in that case can you let him know that he is behaving badly. In that instance. Not a minute later when the digging frenzy passes. Otherwise, Buddy cannot really know what you are truly mad about, can he?

House training an Older Dog

Before you jump straight to teaching Buddy *high-fives* or other fun games so that you can show off your training skills, you need to first prevent your house from becoming an unsanitary environment. And while it is true that house training a puppy is much easier than training an adult dog to go potty, that does not mean that you cannot teach your furry friend where to eliminate waste.

Although it is in their nature not to soil their quarters, dogs that haven't been trained (or haven't been trained successfully) may have established bad habits. In order to break this behavior, you need to go back to the basics, assess the situation, instill healthy habits, and most importantly, be patient.

Getting Ready

Before you try to teach Buddy his new drop zone, you have a few things that you need to take care of, first:

Do a Background Check

If you have adopted your dog just recently, then a background check is indeed in order. You need to find out as much as you can about Buddy's previous upbringing so you can know exactly what you are dealing with and which issues you need to overcome before starting the house training process. Perhaps Buddy was partially house trained in the past. Maybe he was confined for long periods of time on a concrete floor. Maybe he wasn't allowed access to the indoors. There might be some surface preferences for elimination that you need to reset in order to help Buddy get used to the new environment.

Talk to Your Veterinarian

Whether your dog was house trained and has just started eliminating waste in the house or he has bad habits that you need to pull by the root, it is really important to talk to your vet first in order to rule out some underlying medical conditions. You may think that your dog is just stubborn, but he might be dealing with kidney problems or just has an upset tummy due to recent diet changes.

Pay Attention to Buddy's Elimination Habits

In order for you to avoid elimination problems in the future, you first need to know when and where they happen. For instance, if Buddy urinates only on ceramic tiles, you can restrict his access to those rooms, or you can cover the tiles with rugs or towels in order to discourage elimination there so you can start house training and teaching your habits.

Keep Your Home Clean

If your dog is used to having home accidents, then you need to frequently and thoroughly clean the waste odors not only so you can maintain the home hygiene, but also to prevent the odor from encouraging Buddy to eliminate indoors. It is best to try an enzymatic cleaner for this purpose, as they have been known to successfully destroy odors from pet waste. Make sure to also check places that aren't easily reachable such as closets, under the bed, behind the door, etc.

Crate Training (in 1 Weekend)

Before you start the potty-training process, it is important for your dog to be crate trained first. Most dogs are prone to having accidents when left alone. In order to prevent that from happening, the best approach is to confine Buddy to a smaller space when you are not around. And since dogs do not like to soil the place where they sleep and eat, crate training can lay out the perfect foundation for self-control. It's simple really – if Buddy cannot get to the place where he feels free to make a mess, he will be encouraged to 'hold it in.'

Although it sounds like a long and overwhelming process, getting your dog used to the crate can actually be done in a single weekend, which is a great opportunity for busy workers to embark on the dog training train.

The very first thing you need to do is to get the crate ready. Assuming you have already purchased a proper crate that fits your dog's needs, place it in a location that works for you both. If necessary, place some towels or a mat inside to make sure Buddy will be comfortable. Leave the door of the crate open and let Buddy explore.

Then, follow these steps:

Step 1

Friday afternoon, place a couple of doggy treats in the crate. Let them sit there for Buddy to discover. If Buddy enters the crate willingly, mark the behavior the second he steps inside and let him have the reward. If your dog is afraid of getting inside the crate, do not force him to. The worst thing that could happen is for your dog to develop negative feelings toward the crate.

Step 2

Friday night, serve Buddy's dinner in the crate, but make sure to place his bowl closer to the door, not the back of the crate. When Buddy starts eating, start gradually sliding the bowl a bit further into the crate. If he doesn't like to enter completely, give him a few minutes to change his mind. If he loses interest in his dinner, return the bowl a bit closer to the door, but where he still needs to at least place his head inside.

Do not forget to give him a reward after dinner.

Step 3

Saturday morning, start with a more active training. Stand next to his crate and call Buddy. Let Buddy sniff a truly irresistible treat but do not let him have it just yet. Throw the treat inside the crate and wait for his reaction. If he steps inside, immediately say a verbal cue such as **"Bed"** or **"Kennel,"** then mark the behavior and give him another treat.

Repeat this about a dozen times, gradually placing the treat further inside the crate. When Buddy enters the crate completely, give him another treat while he is still there. Then another one. And yet another treat. Finally, top the rewarding with his favorite toy. The point is for Buddy to spend a couple of minutes inside. Then give him a release cue and give him another treat outside of the crate.

Step 4

Later in the morning, repeat the session, only this time, give him the verbal cue before throwing the treat inside. Say **"Kennel"** or whatever word you are using, and with the treat hand, show him the crate. If Buddy goes inside on his own, give him the treat inside and gently close the door. As soon as he eats the treat, let him out.

Repeat this a few times, gradually increasing the length of the time Buddy spends inside with the door closed.

If he is anxious, close the door part way. Make sure to stay positive and to give the verbal cue with an upbeat and cheerful voice.

If Buddy doesn't enter the crate willingly, repeat the previous exercise one more time.

Step 5

Around noon, repeat the same process. Keep increasing the duration until Buddy is comfortable to spend a whole minute inside.

Step 6

Saturday evening, you should start leaving your Bud alone in the crate. Of course, you should try with short periods of time and gradually increase the length. First, practice a few short stays in the crate, with the door closed. Then, close the door and take a couple of steps back. Then take a walk around the room. Do NOT leave the room at this point. Repeat this process about a dozen times. Step away from the crate but make sure that Buddy can still see you.

Step 7

Sunday morning, it is time for longer stays. Ask your dog to go inside the crate and give him something that will keep boredom at bay. His favorite chew toy will do the job. Close the door and let Buddy stay inside the crate for about half an hour or so. Again, do NOT leave the room just yet. Relax on the couch, watch TV, read a book, whatever you do, just don't leave the room. After 30 minutes, give Buddy the release word and let him out. An hour later, repeat the same process.

Tip: Do not lavish Buddy with rewards when he gets out of the crate. Remember, you are training him to love spending time inside the crate, not to be encouraged to get out.

Step 8

In order to make sure that your dog will not get anxious when you leave him alone in the crate and walk out of the room, the best tactic is to make sure that Buddy is tired and will probably need rest. Around noon, give him a really good workout.

Go out for a long walk, play *chase me* in the backyard, go running with Buddy... The point is for your dog to have a long play session so that he can get tired.

Step 9

Give Buddy the cue to go inside the crate, give him a toy he can chew on, and close the door of the crate. Then, leave the room and do not check on Buddy for 10 whole minutes. After ten minutes, go back to the room and use the release word to get Buddy out of the crate. After 10 minutes, repeat the same process. Only this time, leave the room for 15-20 minutes. Repeat this process until you gradually build up to leaving Buddy alone in the crate for a whole hour.

Make sure to give your dog the chance to go potty in between and use the breaks to play and cuddle with your ball of fur to keep anxiety at bay.

Step 10

Early in the evening, it is time for you to actually leave the house. Give buddy the verbal cue to go inside the crate and close the door. Make sure to provide an appropriate chew toy. Then, leave the house and don't go in for 10 minutes. When you get back, let Buddy out, but do not reward or celebrate the fact that he has come out of the crate. After 30 minutes, repeat this again, only this time, leave Buddy in the crate for 20 minutes. Use the release word, open the door, and then go about your evening. Nothing exciting has happened.

Step 11

Early on Monday morning, give Buddy a good workout and make sure he gets tired. Get ready for work, then give him the verbal cue to go inside the crate. Again, make sure to provide a proper chew toy to keep him busy. Then head out, but don't make a fuss about your departure. Make sure to return after a few hours to take Buddy for his midday walk. If your work doesn't allow you to take such a break (or if none of the family members can take Buddy out), then hiring a dog walker is definitely a must. Keep in mind that an adult dog should be left alone in the crate for about 4 hours, but Buddy should absolutely NEVER spend more than 6 hours alone in the crate.

After the weekend training, most dogs should handle well spending a few hours alone in the crate. If you think that your dog is overly anxious, consult with your veterinarian.

Going Potty

With a puppy, you have a blank slate. It is you who sets the foundation for good behavior, so you can say that it is easy to teach him to go potty. With an adult dog, things are different. Older dogs have already established elimination habits. Your job is to rewrite that chapter and help them adopt healthier habits. And while that seems like a lot of work, the good thing about teaching a dog to go potty is that adult dogs learn quickly. Most older dogs can be potty trained in less than a week.

Make the Time

Dogs learn quickly, yes, but it is you who has to find the time for training. It is best if you could take a few days off work so you can focus on the training process. The routine here is of extreme importance, so make sure to provide consistency.

Establish the Area

Your dog needs to have a specific drop zone where he can eliminate waste. It is highly recommended that his drop zone is outdoors, but not too far from your home so you can conveniently take him there every time he needs to go.

If you live in a house and have a backyard, then you can designate a special area in your yard for this purpose. If you live in a high-rise apartment or if you are unable to provide outdoor access that easily, in that case, paper training your dog is recommended.

Escort!

If you have a backyard and your dog was partially potty trained, then you are probably used to just opening the door and letting him go outside to do his business. To retrain him properly, you have to actually take him there yourself. If your dog was not house trained at all before, even better. Just make sure to escort him to the designated spot, on a leash.

Use the Verbal Cue

Once you are at the desired elimination zone, wait for Buddy to do his business. Pay attention to his movements and the second you see him urinating or defecating, say **"Go Potty"** or whatever cue works best for you. Immediately after Buddy is done, reward him with a yummy treat.

Repeat this every time he goes potty, for as long as it takes for him to go on cue whenever you are at the drop zone (assuming that you already know his potty schedule well and that you are sure he actually needs to go, of course).

Rely on Consistency

The key to successful house training lies in having a consistent feeding and potty routine. It is pretty simple, really. The more regular his feeding is, the more regular Buddy will eliminate waste. Be consistent with his feeding times, as well as the amount of food that is recommended for his age and/or unique medical condition. Consult with your vet and stick to that schedule.

Once you establish consistent feeding, it will be much easier for you to pinpoint when Buddy will feel the urge to eliminate. Most healthy dogs need to go every few hours, but after a couple of days of consistent feeding, you will be able to find out when those times are so you can take Buddy out then, in order to avoid accidents.

Avoid Accidents

The goal is for Buddy to have as few accidents at home as possible. Of course, you can prevent this with a consistent routine, but it is impossible to strictly plan his physiological needs. Pay attention to signs that Buddy needs to go. Most dogs start circling and whining when they have the need to go, so if you see that or if your dog suddenly starts sniffing and pacing, then attach his leash and immediately take him to his drop zone outside.

Also, make sure to put away his water bowl before bedtime so that you can prevent him from urinating at home during the night. Don't worry. If Buddy is really thirsty, he will let you know. This is obviously not recommended if Buddy had a lot of exercise at night or if it is too hot at home.

Do NOT Punish

If you see that Buddy has made an accident, do not yell at him or punish him in any way. The old fashioned newspaper roll is not only cruel and inhumane but highly ineffective as well. Clean the accident and follow the tips from above to prevent it from happening again.

If you, however, catch Buddy during the act, midstream, just clap your hand or say a negative word such as **"Oops"** in order to startle him. Then put on his leash and take him to his drop zone. Say **"Go Potty"** and wait for him to do his business there. Once he eliminates, reward the good behavior.

Even if Buddy doesn't have the need to go anymore, it is still beneficial to take him outside to the elimination spot so he can see the connection between the *"Oops"* with the *"Go Potty"* and his drop zone, in order to understand that he has made a mistake.

What If Buddy Takes Forever to Go?

If Buddy needs a lot of time to go every time he is taken to the drop zone, it is probably because he is *hanging on*. Most dogs do that after they associate the *"Go Potty"* with being returned home. Do not take him straight home after he has done his business. Reward him and praise him like crazy, then spend some time playing with him outside or take him for a walk. Repeat this for a couple of days and soon enough, Buddy will start going on cue as he will be keen to go potty thanks to the fact that it results with treats and games.

Keep in Mind: Old dogs need to eliminate waste more frequently than younger, healthier dogs. That is not a result of unsuccessful training but happens because Buddy cannot hold the waste as long. If that is the case, you might want to consider providing a place inside your home where Buddy can go potty when you are not home or engage a neighbor that can help out.

Paper Training

To paper train your dog means to teach him to eliminate waste on a small, designated spot in your home, that is covered with a special pad, mat, or even a pile of newspapers. This is not recommended for healthy dogs and owners that have the ability to provide a consistent potty routine outside. However, if you live in a high-rise apartment downtown, if you have a very busy schedule, if Buddy has difficulty going outside, or if you are in no condition to get your dog there, then paper training can be of great benefit to you and your furry friend.

Select the Potty Area

The very first thing you need to do is to choose a potty area inside your home that works for you. Give this a good thought as you will be training your dog to go potty there, permanently. So, where are you comfortable for Buddy to eliminate waste? Think about it well. The tile floor in the kitchen may be the easiest to clean, but do you really want Buddy to be soiling this area?

Keep in mind that Buddy will have to be confined to this area while you are not home, so choose wisely.

Line the Area

Line the area where you want Buddy to eliminate waste with special puppy pads, a mat that can soak up the urine, or even by arranging a pile of newspapers there. Choose whatever works for you and what you can afford, but keep in mind that special puppy pads are more absorbent and leave almost no mess behind.

Just make sure to provide a lot of space in the beginning, so that Buddy can associate the pads with his urge to eliminate waste.

Encourage Buddy to Use Them

Around his potty times, place Buddy on top of the pads and wait for him to eliminate. The instant he starts doing that, say **"Pad"** or **"Potty"** or whatever cue you want to use. Once he is done, reward him. Repeat this for as long as it takes for him to learn that he should do his business on the pads.

If Buddy doesn't want to step onto the pads, physically place him there or lure him onto the pads with a yummy treat.

Reduce

Once Buddy begins eliminating waste onto the lined area, you will have to start gradually reducing the size of it. You wouldn't want your Buddy to use half of your room as a drop zone now, would you? Most owners are comfortable with their dog eliminating waste in a small area in some corner of their house (just like a litter box for cats), so ideally, you should aim for that.

Each day, reduce the size by a 1/8 or so until you get to a suitable size.

Encourage Some More

You need to continue encouraging Buddy to use that area, even if he is confused. At first, he might just try to eliminate where those pads used to be. If you catch him trying to eliminate outside of that area, say **"Oops"** and clap your hands. Then immediately take Buddy to the area and give him the verbal cue **"Potty"** or **"Pad."** Keep rewarding and praising the good behavior to encourage him to repeat it.

What If Buddy is Struggling?

Keep in mind that dogs progress differently. If you see that Buddy is seriously struggling, take a step back. Increase the area by a ¼ and let Buddy get more comfortable with eliminating waste there. Give it some more time and then reduce again.

Teaching Behavior in 4 Weeks

In order for your dog to start listening to you, you first have to teach him your language. Doing so will not only result in mutual understanding but it will also be a great opportunity for you to become a bit more fluent in Buddy's language, as well. Being able to easily understand each others needs and wants will take your communication and connection to a higher level, which will, in turn, enable you to embark on a fun adventure that will empower you both equally.

This chapter represents the core of this book as it contains the mechanics of an effective dog training program. In theory, the content of this chapter represents about 4 weeks' worth of training. However, don't be disappointed if you cannot convince Buddy to get off your couch in time for the next session. The four-week plan is really just a plan. Nothing is set in stone, so feel free to take as much time as you need, or even fast-forward if your dog is a canine prodigy. The main point of this chapter is not to obsess over getting your dog to behave in less than a month but to lay out the foundation for Buddy's future.

Where to Train Buddy?

Many new dog owners think that the nearest park will be the perfect place for them to start training their dogs. But what they don't know is that going outside immediately sets them on the path to failure. If your dog hasn't been able to learn proper manners for whatever reason and is used to doing whatever pleases him, you will have a pretty hard time taming him when he gets wired up by outer distractions.

Keep in mind that you should take baby steps and start from the very beginning. Your dog probably doesn't even respond to his own name yet; what makes you think that you can handle the presence of other dogs, bikes passing through, birds, squirrels, and all that outdoor noise? The best place to start training Buddy is inside the house.

Start the training inside and make sure to do it when there are minimal distractions. For instance, if you have a hyperactive toddler jumping around the house, do the training when he is taking a nap.

If you always use the same room for training, your dog will be less and less distracted and will eventually learn to put his sole focus on you. However, as beneficial as this is for teaching a new behavior, keep in mind that once Buddy learns a skill, you should take it somewhere else.

Otherwise, your dog might mistakenly associate the behavior with, for instance, an object in that room. For example, if you do the training in the garage and Buddy is used to sitting down next to your toolbox, giving him the "Sit" command in the living room may not work. He will probably become confused as there will be no toolbox for him to sit down next to. This will most likely make you believe that your dog is stubborn, when in fact, it is a training mistake you are dealing with. Many dog owners make this mistake, so make sure that, once Buddy learns a skill, you start practicing it in different places.

The Basic Formula

Teaching your dog a new behavior requires a simple but consistent formula. This 5-step process will help you instill proper discipline and teach Buddy good manners. Just stick to this rule and success is guaranteed:

1: Get the dog's behavior.

Whether you capture, shape, or lure the behavior, the very first step is to get your Bud to perform the desired behavior.

2: Mark the behavior.

Whether you choose the clicker or you simply tell Buddy "Good boy" immediately after the performed action, marking the behavior is of crucial importance for the training process as it helps the dog instantly get that what he has done is good and that the reward is coming.

3: Give Buddy a reward for the performed action.

The best way to get your dog to learn the desired behavior is to motivate him to repeat it again in the future. By using a yummy treat, favorite toy, granting outdoor access, or some other reward that your dog will enjoy the most, the point is to help him learn that the performed behavior is good and rewarding.

4: Add a verbal cue before the action is performed so that Buddy can associate the command with the correct behavior.

In order for your dog to successfully associate the proper behavior with the right command, you need to give the verbal cue just before the action is performed. For instance, you say "Sit" when you see that Buddy is about to sit down. Asking him to do it when he is not offering the behavior easily may only cause confusion, and worse, you risk teaching him that the word "Sit" means "ignore me and go play with your squeaky toy."

5: Use the verbal command to elicit the appropriate behavior.

Once your dog becomes familiar with the verbal command and its meaning, you can then start using the cue first, in order to elicit the correct action. Just keep in mind that in order for the training to be successful, you need to have Buddy's undivided attention, so make sure that your ball of fur is actually focused on you before starting.

Week 1 Training

Training an adult dog is very different than training a young puppy. You'd think that it's easier since a grown-up dog can perform many different tasks with ease, but the truth is, the older your dog is, the trickier it is for you to direct him in the right way. And, if your dog is used to getting things his way, training him can sound like an especially daunting chore to you. However, if you start things from the very beginning, even the most stubborn ball of fur can learn proper behavior in less than a month.

The first week should be for the most basic commands and simple behavior. Do not try to tackle more advanced training programs because your dog already knows how to sit. If Buddy hasn't had a training class in his life, all of this can be new to him. In order to keep him interested, you have to avoid asking too much in return. Just follow this carefully crafted training program and keep his enthusiasm high throughout the process.

What's Your Name?

Knowing his name is the very first thing that your dog has to learn. And I do not mean just for the sake of avoiding an identity crisis. Giving you his full attention whenever you call his name can save you a lot of trouble in the future. The goal of this training exercise is to teach your dog that hearing his name means "drop everything and look at me."

When teaching your older dog his name, the key to success is to say it as often as possible, and not only when you need him to give you his attention, but pretty much every time you talk to him. Just make sure not to get frustrated if your dog needs a little bit more time to master this lesson. This is especially important in case you've adopted an abandoned dog, as he probably needs some extra persuading in order to start cooperating.

Here is how you can name-train your dog:

1. Get ready by ensuring that you are in a distraction-free place where your dog can give you his full attention. Place a couple of tasty treats in your pocket for rewarding.

2. Sit down with your dog and make sure that you have his attention. You can brush him, give him a massage, or just talk to him for a while. The point is for your dog to be focused on you before saying his name out loud.

3. Say his name and mark the behavior. This is best done with a clicker, but you can also mark it with a smooching sound or a clap.

4. Immediately give him the reward.

5. Repeat this process a dozen times. The point is for your Buddy to associate the sound of his name with the reward, in order to remember to look at you whenever he hears you calling him.

6. Now that you've been playing this game for a while, it is time to test your Buddy's attention. Wait until your dog looks away. Then, say his name to check if he has already started associating his name with the reward. Buddy's head should snap back toward your direction when he hears his name. If it does, mark the behavior immediately and give him a treat. If not, practice saying his name when he is focused on you a bit longer before testing him again.

Play a Game!

When your dog begins getting the gist of the exercise, you can pay a game involving all of the members in your family:

1. Give everyone a couple of treats and gather around in a semicircle.

2. Say Buddy's name. When he looks at you, mark the behavior with a clap, a click, or by saying "Good boy," and give him a treat.

3. Have someone else say Buddy's name. Take turns saying his name. Just remember to instantly mark and reward the behavior.

This is a fun way for Buddy to practice and learn the meaning of his name.

What If Buddy Is not Responding?

If your dog doesn't look at you when you say his name, even after spending a decent amount of training, then perhaps you need to make some changes. In most cases, the dog doesn't respond because he is not motivated to play along or because he is preoccupied with something that's more interesting to him. Try to take the training somewhere with fewer distractions and change the reward. For instance, if you're using regular doggy food, treat him with something a bit more tempting. If that doesn't seem to do the trick, then schedule the training before his meals. Training him on an empty stomach may motivate him to play along just to get the treat.

Also, you could try marking the behavior with some exciting sounds like the squeak of his favorite toy. If Buddy is still unresponsive, then perhaps you need to have his hearing checked. But don't worry. Even if your dog is hearing-impaired, there are a lot of different ways for you to mark the behavior. A fun vibrating collar and a light beam are just a couple of great options.

Teaching Him to Sit

"Sit" is the most basic command, and besides their name, usually the first one that dogs master. Besides the fact that getting your dog to sit down can be useful in various situations, mastering this command is also the beginning of establishing a strong bond with Buddy. Make sure to make the session enjoyable.

1. Fill your pockets with tasty treats and go to the designated training area.

2. Hang out there with Buddy and wait until he sits down. When he puts his bottom to the ground, immediately click, or make the marking sound, and give him the treat.

3. Wait for him to sit down again and repeat the process a dozen times.

4. Once your dog begins understanding the connection between the behavior and the treat, you should start eliciting the action with the verbal command.

5. Stand in front of your dog with a treat in your hand. Make sure he notices it so that you'll have his full attention.

6. Place the treat near his nose and gently raise it above his head. Chances are, your dog will keep his eyes locked on the treat and follow it with his nose. Then, lower the treat down to the ground.

7. When you notice that Buddy is about to sit down, give him the **"Sit"** command.

8. Once he is down, mark the good behavior and give him the treat.

9. Repeat this for about 10 minutes or so, but don't push too hard. If you notice your dog looking away or sniffing around, he is most likely bored. Take a break and resume another time. If you're training consistently, your dog will most likely catch on after only a week.

What If the Dog is Very Active?

If you are dealing with an especially rambunctious dog, then the previous method may not work so well. Dogs that are very active will most likely just jump around at the sight of the treat. Getting them to sit down can be a true challenge. For that purpose, you will probably need to offer physical guidance in order to have better control over Buddy:

1. Put Buddy on a leash. He needs to be able to stay in place in order to give you his attention. By putting him on a leash, you will have him close to your side.

2. Stand next to your dog. You will need to lower him to a sitting position physically, so give Buddy a gentle push above his rear legs.

3. Just before Buddy puts his bottom to the ground, say **"Sit."**

4. Mark the behavior immediately and give him a treat.

5. Repeat this for a day or two, then try the sitting command again, but without using your hand on Buddy's back. The point is for Buddy to associate the command with the behavior and the behavior with the reward.

What If Buddy Refuses to Offer a Sit?

If your dog is not interested in sitting down on cue, you will probably have to spend some more time teaching him the connection between the behavior and the reward. Whenever you see him sitting down, say "Sit," and immediately give him a treat.

Another thing you can try is to practice the sit command when your dog is a bit tired. Go for a walk or play a game of fetch before the training session in order to get him pooped and encourage him to sit down.

Come Happens

Most dog trainers agree that "Come" is one of the most important commands that your dog has to master. Also known as *recall*, "come" will give your dog the freedom to walk off-leash and provide him with endless exploring opportunities to shake off that extra energy. Mastering this technique will give you peace of mind that your dog will come to you when called, which will be of enormous importance when Buddy decides that chasing a squirrel across the road is a fun way to spend the afternoon.

But, before we start with the steps to teaching him this command, it is important to mention that you should pay attention not to *poison the cue*. You cannot be teaching Buddy to come to you when called and give him rewards for it and then tell him to go away when he comes to you while you are trying to take an afternoon nap. In order for Buddy to truly master the "Come" command, you need to make him feel that coming to you is something positive and rewarding. Never punish him for coming to you just because you are not in the mood for it.

Also, do not use the "Come" command when you want to cut the walk short, clip his nails, give him a bath, or do something that Buddy doesn't enjoy. You need to help him associate "Come" with positivity, not with the fact that his play time might be over.

Here are simple instructions that will teach your Bud to come to you in no time:

1. Fill your pockets with treats and get your dog in the same room as you. Stand near him, then turn and run away from him.

2. If Buddy starts running towards you, say **"Come"** immediately, then mark the behavior and give your dog the treat when he approaches you. If he isn't too excited to make a move, see if you can encourage him to follow you by making a smooching noise or squeaking a toy. The point is to get Buddy excited in order to follow you.

3. Once Buddy starts running to you every time you give him the command, you should decrease your movement and get him to come to you even when you are standing still.

4. Do not take "Come" outside just yet. If you are not at least 90 percent sure that Buddy will come to you when called, it is way too early for you to take him off the leash. Practice this command inside your house or in the comfort of your backyard for as long

as it takes for Buddy to understand that hearing the word "come" means to come to you willingly.

What If Buddy Isn't Interested in Following You?

If you are dealing with a very unenthusiastic dog, then it is possible that your ball of fur will lose interest in following you after the first couple attempts. If that happens, do not despair. You just have to start the training at a much slower pace; that's it. If Buddy isn't particularly excited to come to you willingly, then the best way to train him on this command is while he is on the leash.

1. Leash Buddy. In order for you to keep him close and make sure that he is focused on you, attach a shorter leash to his collar.

2. Grab some doggy treats, pick up the leash and stand just a couple of steps away from your dog.

3. Show him the treat as you take a step backward. Start taking backward steps and wait for Buddy to come your way. When he starts following you, say **"Come."**

4. Keep moving backward slowly, until your dog reaches you. When that happens, immediately mark the behavior, give him the reward, and praise him like crazy.

5. Do this a couple of times, then reduce the distance to a single step backward. The goal is to be able to get Buddy to come to you without taking any steps. When that happens, you can start practicing this command off the leash.

Keep it Fun!

In order to teach your dog that "*come*" is a positive thing, you need to help him associate the command with excitement. And the best way to do so is to make sure that the training sessions are fun and enjoyable for him.

Round-Robin. Once Buddy begins responding to the "*come*" command successfully, you can add an extra dash of complexity by playing a fun and challenging game. Invite 2-3 friends or family members to stand in a circle, about twenty feet apart from each other. Give them a few small treats and let each of them issue the "*come*" command. When Buddy comes to them, let them mark the behavior and give him the treat.

Hide and Seek. Practicing the "*come*" command regularly, even if Buddy comes to you willingly, is of great importance. To keep it fun, set aside 10 minutes to play hide and seek with your dog every once in a while. After Buddy has mastered the skill, hide in another room and issue the command. Let Buddy find you and come to you. Once he does that, lavish him with treats and praises.

What If Buddy Isn't Cooperative at All?

If you have adopted an older dog and have trouble teaching him the "*come*" command, it is possible that Buddy has developed an aversion to that verbal cue. Perhaps, he has learned that the word "*come*" means that it's time to go home and thinks that he is about to get punished, so he doesn't like to cooperate.

Sometimes, dogs also associate this command with a game of chase if the word "*come*" has been used a lot around playtime. If you cannot get your dog to come to you, try using a different command word instead. "Here" is another option that many trainers use instead of "come."

Down!

If you are annoyed by the fact that your ball of fur has to drool on the lap of your visitors, then this command will surely put a stop to it. But that is not the only reason why "*Down*" can be of great importance.

Imagine this scenario: You are walking with your dog off leash when all of a sudden you see him trying to catch the cat he's just spotted across the street. You see a car coming his way, and concerned for his well-being, you shout "*Down.*" Your dog drops on the sidewalk and you have just enough time to grab Buddy's collar and attach his leash to it. The upside of "*Down*" in these situations is that, unlike "*Sit,*" you are given more time to catch your furry friend as it takes a bit more effort to raise from a "*Down*" position.

Whether you are concerned about his safety, want to stop him from annoying your guests, or you simply want him lying quietly in a café so that you can have your morning coffee in peace, here is how you can teach Buddy the "*Down*" command quickly.

The best (and fastest) strategy is to lure your dog into the "*down*" position instead of waiting for him to lie down on his own. But, in order to do so, you will have to command him to *sit* first.

That means that in order for Buddy to master "*down,*" he should already have a great understanding of the "*sit*" command. Make sure to start this training only after your dog can learn how to sit on cue.

1. With some treats in your hand, give your dog the "*sit*" command. When he sits down, gently pat him to acknowledge the good behavior, but do not click or mark the behavior as you usually do. Do not give him the treat just yet. This is important as marking the behavior will give Buddy the signal that he is done performing the desired action, and you may end up losing his attention.

2. Let Buddy see the treat and put it near his nose. Gently lower it to the ground. When you notice Buddy's elbows are about to touch the ground, and he is preparing to lie down, give the **"Down"** command.

3. Once he is fully to the ground, mark the behavior, and give him the treat immediately.

4. Repeat this about a dozen times before using the verbal cue to elicit the behavior. Once Buddy learns what "Down" means, you are ready to ask for it. Simply say "Down" and wait for the response. If Buddy lies down immediately, then he has already understood the meaning of the exercise. Mark his behavior and lavish him with rewards. If he doesn't do anything, use your empty hand to lure him to the "*down*" position. If that doesn't help either, then you are probably moving too fast. Go back and repeat the steps 1-3 until your dog really catches on.

What If Buddy Stands Up?

It is not uncommon for some dogs to stand up instead of lying down when the treat is lowered to the ground. If that happens, pay attention to how you are lowering the treat. If you are not moving your hand straight down and the treat sort of goes away from his head, your dog will probably get up to follow it. If that is not the issue, however, then you should probably *shape* the command.

Just when your dog starts moving his head to follow the treat, mark the good behavior by using the clicker or making the usual sign. That way, Buddy will understand better that moving toward the floor is what earns the treat.

What If Buddy is Stubborn and Won't Get Down?

If shaping doesn't help Buddy get down either, then you are perhaps dealing with a very stubborn dog. Training a dog that just won't do as you say can be frustrating, but equally successful. All you need is to add a dash of creativity in order to spark Buddy's enthusiasm and motivate him to participate. Here is a creative way to get your Bud down:

1. Sit on the floor next to Buddy, but keep one of your knees high, allowing enough space for him to crawl under it.

2. Lure Buddy to your knee by putting a tasty treat under it. He will have to get down to take it. As soon as you see his elbows touching the ground, say **"Down."**

3. When he lies down completely, mark the behavior immediately, and give him the treat.

If this doesn't help either, then perhaps it is best to give it some time and train Buddy by capturing his behavior. Wait for him to lie down on his own. The moment you notice that he is about to lower his elbows to the ground, say "Down." Then mark, and reward. Repeat this for as long as it takes for him to catch on what the verbal cue means.

Week 2 Training

Now that you have spent a whole week teaching Buddy how to sit, lie down, and come to you, it is time to add a few more words to his dictionary. It is okay if your dog still hasn't learned some of the last week's commands. You can proceed with the training program even if Buddy doesn't quite get how to lie down on cue yet. Just make sure to continue practicing the command he hasn't mastered yet during the second week as well.

Stand!

Okay, you probably will not use the "*stand*" command as often as "*down*" or "*sit.*" However, teaching your dog to stand can be of great importance, especially for wiping muddy paws, grooming, vet checks, or simply preventing him from sitting in a muddy puddle.

The best thing about "*Stand*" is that it's perhaps one of the easiest commands to teach, and dogs catch on this concept pretty quickly.

Here is how you can get your Bud to hold a standing position:

1. Instruct your dog to sit in front of you. You should be about one foot away from Buddy.

2. Hold a treat in your hand and lift it in front of his nose, about a few inches away. Then, gently start pulling it upwards. Chances are your dog will stand up to follow it.

3. The moment you notice he is about to stand up, say **"Stand."**

4. Once he is up, click or mark the behavior immediately and give him the treat. If you want your Bud to stand longer, you can let him nibble on the doggy treat while holding the position.

Practice this about a dozen times or so, until your dog learns what "*stand*" means. Then, you can lure your dog to a standing position while you slowly back away from him. As soon as he is up, say **"Stand"** as you move. If he remains in that position, mark the behavior immediately, and reward him. If not, repeat the steps 1-4 for another dozen times until he really catches on.

The goal here is to fade your movements gradually, until Buddy is able to "*stand*" when he hears the command, without being lured with a treat.

What If Buddy Doesn't Stand Up?

If your dog isn't interested in getting up to follow the treat and just sits there lazily, hoping that you will give it to him, then he is probably not motivated enough. Get creative to entice excitement. Start acting silly, squeak his favorite toy, make funny noises, try jumping up and down… Do whatever it is you think will excite Buddy to stand up. When he is finally in a standing position, mark and reward, to motivate him to repeat the behavior again.

Wait a Second

Saying "Wait" should be just as pressing the *pause* button. It should be a command that will tell your dog to pause for a second and not follow you. It can also serve as a reminder for Buddy that he should defer to you. So, you are not only teaching general behavior here, but you are also instilling good manners.

The most common use of "*wait*" is when the dog owner is about to go out the door and does not want his dog all wired up, thinking he is about to step out into the wonderland too. Because that's what dogs do; they get so excited when they see your hand on the doorknob, that calming them afterward becomes a real headache.

You would think that teaching your overly active dog to *"Wait"* is nearly impossible, but the truth is that this command is one of the easiest to teach. Why? Because you have the best opportunity to train him. How? Since Buddy probably goes in and out of the house a couple of times a day, he can quickly learn that when he *"waits"* for you to open the door first, he gets rewarded by going outside.

1. Go to your front door and instruct your dog to come. Do not take or show the leash to him.

2. Once your dog has joined you in the entryway, wait for him to sit down. You can also instruct him to do so, but the point here is to get him to offer the behavior himself, without being asked.

3. When he finally sits down, say **"Wait"** and make a hand signal to enforce the behavior by putting your hand in front of his nose, with the palm facing him.

4. Now, slowly reach for the doorknob with your hand, and before touching it, mark the behavior either with a clicker, a sound, or simply saying "Good Boy," and give Buddy a yummy treat. If your dog moves before you get the chance to mark the behavior, use a negative word such as **"Oops,"** show him the treat, but do not give it to him. Your dog should learn that he gets rewarded only for good behavior. Wait for him to sit down on his own and repeat the same step until his behavior deserves the treat.

5. Repeat steps 1-3. This time, instead of only reaching for the doorknob, open it just a crack. Mark the behavior immediately and give Buddy a treat.

6. Again, repeat the first three steps. Now, open the door wider. If Buddy is still waiting, mark and reward. If not, say the negative word and give him the no-reward mark.

7. Gradually open the door wider, until you can step outside and close the door. Once you manage to do that with Buddy still waiting, open the door immediately, go back inside, mark and reward.

The best reward here would be letting your dog out the door as that is what he has been patiently waiting for the whole time, after all. Repeat this a couple of times during the day. Step outside and invite him through after he has been a good boy. Then, play a game of fetch with him in your backyard, take him for a walk, a ride in the car, or do something that Buddy will truly enjoy as a reward.

Caution: If your front door leads directly to the street, practice this method with a safe door. If you have a backyard, your back door can be perfect for this training. If not, place his favorite toys in your bedroom or another room in the house, let him see that, and then close the door. Let Buddy wait in front of the door and try this method there. After he has patiently waited for you to open the door completely and step into the room, invite him in and reward him with a fun game.

What If Buddy Isn't Interested in What's on the Other Side of the Door?

If you cannot get your dog to sit and give you a minute of his attention, or even worse, if he just wanders off and isn't at all interested in what you are trying to reward him with, then perhaps you have lost the battle with the environment. See if you can lower the distractions so you can ensure that Buddy will put his focus on you, try luring him with tastier treats, better toys, etc. or at the end, just leash him. Obviously, you're not supposed to tug on the collar to force him to participate, but a gentle restraint can be quite beneficial in keeping his eyes on the prize.

No Pulling, Mister!

So, you've finally managed to get your dog to accept the collar around his neck and the light pressure of the leash, only to discover that you are nowhere near taking Buddy for a calm walk around the block. Getting your Bud to walk calmly on a leash is perhaps the most challenging thing when it comes to dog training.

It is in your dog's nature to be curious. Dogs want to explore the endless varieties of sights and scents, so running around sniffing and chasing things, to them, is what they are supposed to do when out for a walk. Your dog is born to pull. He probably finds you slow, boring, and since pulling on the leash gets him where he wants to go much faster, he sees nothing wrong in dragging you around the park.

However, even though it may be one of their basic instincts, you shouldn't tolerate it. For Buddy, pulling gets him wherever he wants to go. To put it simply, allowing him to navigate you gets him rewarded.

Perform these steps to teach your dog how not to pull on the leash:

1. Attach the leash to Buddy's collar and go to a place where there aren't many distractions, and where you will be able to walk in a circle or in a straight line. Have some treats in your pocket.

2. Take the leash with your right hand and put the loop over your thumb. Now, make a fist. Keep your left hand placed just under your right hand, holding the leash with both of your hands. Your hands should be placed as if you were holding a baseball bat.

3. Give him a verbal cue such as **"Let's Go"** or **"Let's Walk,"** and start walking.

4. Just before he gets the chance to get to the other end of the leash and start pulling on it, say **"Easy,"** and immediately make an about-turn to the right, in order to start walking in the opposite direction.

    TIP: Hold the leash firmly, but keep in mind that if you keep your entire right hand in through the loop, Buddy might surprise you and make you fall. The loop should be kept over your thumb at all times, so if needed, you can straighten your hand and let it slide off.

5. By holding the leash like you would a baseball bat, and turning in the opposite direction, you are providing a slight pressure on Buddy's collar and prompting him to turn in the new direction.

6. As Buddy is catching up to you, mark the behavior immediately and give him a treat for being such a good boy.

What If Buddy is Just Leaning into His Collar?

If your dog is already leaning into the collar, then you are probably late with your command. Go back to the beginning and make sure you are concentrated. You need to pay attention to how you are giving the cue, the way in which you are holding the leash, but also, you need to learn to anticipate when to make the turn. Watch Buddy and make sure he is focused as well. Be sure to give him the *"Easy"* command first, as this is the cue that you want him to slow down and not to pull. To keep him enthusiastic about the training, provide variety in the rewards and don't let him become bored.

What If Buddy Is Too Strong?

If your dog is too strong and you cannot restrain him, you need to consider getting a different collar in order to prevent him from dragging you around the block. Many trainers say that front-clip no-pull harnesses are the best choice for this purpose. Unlike regular harnesses, these models that have the front clip prevent the dog from pulling that much, as they are designed to turn the dog toward the walker when they begin pulling on the leash.

What If Buddy Pulls Back on the Leash?

In most cases, untrained dogs go in front of the walkers, pulling on the leash and directing them to go whenever they feel like it. However, in some cases, the dog may be pulling back on the leash. This is a sign of fearfulness, which is not uncommon for abandoned or abused dogs. If you've recently adopted your dog or don't know his history, do not rule out that possibility. If this is the case, do not force your dog to learn the no-pull method too quickly as that can only backfire. Instead, work on building up their confidence and strengthening your relationship.

1. Stand near your dog with treats in your hand and wait for him to come to you voluntarily. Mark the behavior and give him a giant reward. Do this about a dozen times or so.

2. Next, when Buddy comes to you, take out a treat, let him sniff it, but do not give it to him just yet. With the treat in your hand, slowly start walking. Make a couple of steps and then mark the behavior and give Buddy the treat. Repeat this a dozen times.

3. Once you notice Buddy becoming less scared of walking next to you, repeat step 2, only this time, hold the leash like a baseball bat. If Buddy starts to pull back on it, work on step 2 some more. If not, keep walking, marking, and rewarding as you go.

If your dog is fearful, he will probably not pull on the leash. However, he may try to make multiple stops. When that happens, apply gentle pressure on the leash to remind Buddy that you should keep going. Once he takes a step forward, mark, and reward.

The Touch

Touch is the same as targeting. It is basically teaching Buddy to touch a target with his nose, on your command, whether it is the door, some object, or your hand. This is more of a game than it is a behavior, but once you start teaching it to your dog, you will see how much fun it is for him. It is almost like pushing a button; you touch something with your nose, you get a yummy treat. What's not to like?

But, besides being a great way to show off your training skills, the "*touch*" command can also be quite helpful if you are dealing with a stubborn dog who doesn't always listen to you when you tell him to *come*. "*Touch*" is way more enjoyable, and even when the dog doesn't feel like coming to you when you tell him to, giving him the "*touch*" command will most likely change his mind.

"*Touch*" is perfect for the second week of training when you are beginning to teach more challenging behavior. The training will feel like a game and will keep overwhelm at bay.

For "*touch*," you can use pretty much any object. However, I strongly recommend starting with your hand as the target. Your Buddy loves sniffing your hands so it will be much faster and easier to teach him this behavior if you use your hand.

1. Have yummy treats (and the clicker, if you are using one) in one hand. Make sure that the other hand is empty as that will be the target.

2. Stand in front of your dog and gently place your hand near his nose. Your fingers should be pointed down. Wait for him to sniff it. Once he touches your hand with his nose, mark the behavior, and give him a treat. Repeat this a couple of times in order for Buddy to understand that touching your hand is what gets him rewarded.

3. Repeat the first two steps, only this time, as Buddy prepares to touch your palm with his nose, you say **"Touch."** Then, mark and reward. Practice this a couple of times.

4. Once Buddy gets familiar with the "*touch*" command, you can start moving the target. Back away from your dog and see if he will follow it. Place it in different angles at nose level. Once he becomes more confident, you can try placing the target on the floor, a bit higher, etc.

When Buddy masters the "*touch*" behavior with your hand, you can then try it with different objects.

What If Buddy Doesn't Touch Your Hand?

If Buddy is confused and is not interested at all in touching your palm with his nose, it is perhaps because your other hand distracts him. Make sure to keep your hand with the treats (and clicker) behind your back so that Buddy can only see your empty hand.

If that is not the issue, then try to entice him to sniff and touch your hand. Rub a treat on your target hand before offering it to him. If this does the trick, repeat it for as long as it takes for Buddy to master "*touch*." However, make sure to gradually fade out the scent in order to avoid Bud from becoming dependent on the yummy aroma.

Week 3 Training

During the third week, you will most likely notice significant progress in the way in which Buddy responds to the training sessions. If you have been following this book's instructions right, then he already knows the basic commands and gets pretty enthusiastic to get the behavior right in the hope of getting a yummy reward.

This is the time when you should introduce more advanced techniques and take his behavior to a whole new level. Of course, you should also continue practicing the commands that he is already familiar with, but make sure to gradually increase the environmental distractions (having the cat in the same room, doing it in the backyard with your toddler running around, etc.) so that you can prepare him for uncertainties in the real world and teach him how to respond to your commands the right way during these situations.

Walk Nicely by My Side

When it comes to dog walking, most dog owners confuse heeling with being able to walk on a loose leash. And while the latter is a skill that your dog absolutely has to have mastered in order for you to take him out for a nice walk, there are times when you will simply need him to "*heel*."

Heeling means walking on your left side, on your command. It is very different than loose leash walking when Buddy is on his own, sniffing around and chasing pigeons. When he is at your heel, your dog focuses on you every step of the way. He walks nicely by your side, whether you make a left turn, slow down, or decide to run. Heeling is a behavior that will be greatly appreciated when walking on a crowded and busy sidewalk or at times when you will need to have absolute control. If you are planning to sign up Buddy for obedience competition, keep in mind that he must master the "*heel*" command first.

But, before you jump straight to teaching your Buddy how to walk nicely by your side, you should first introduce sitting at heel, in order for your dog to get the handle of this command and become familiar with it. Here is how you can do it:

1. Place some treats in your pocket. Attach Buddy's leash to his collar and instruct him to sit down. Make sure that he is sitting on your left side, and that you are both facing in the same direction. Put the leash over your shoulder. It is best to have Buddy sitting down on your left side and his leash placed over your right shoulder

2. With your right foot, take one step forward. Then, take a step with your left foot but make sure to put the left foot past your right. Drop your right knee down and place your hand on Buddy's chest. Gently fold him to readjust his position from sitting to sitting at heel, saying **"Heel"** in a firm but positive tone, at the same time.

3. Immediately mark the behavior and give him a treat.

4. Keep in mind that Buddy knows how to sit, you just need to show him where you want him to do it. Repeat for as long as it takes for Buddy to understand what "*heel*" means. Just make sure not to push on his rear end, and each time you're saying "*heel*," gradually decrease the physical assistance, giving Buddy the chance to catch on and eventually do this on his own.

Now that Buddy knows where he is supposed to go when he hears the word "*heel,*" it is time for you to teach him to actually walk at heel. To do so, perform these steps:

1. Attach Buddy's leash to his collar. Instruct him to sit at heel, again, you should both be facing the same direction. Place the leash over your right shoulder, but make sure to allow some slack (about 4 inches or so) to ensure that there will be no tension on his collar when you start walking.

2. With your hands close to your body and at waist height, make a funnel around the leash. The point of this is so you can avoid touching the leash when there is no need for it.

3. Give the **"Heel"** command in a firm but positive tone and start walking in a brisk way. The pace here is really important as your goal is to prompt Buddy to take a step forward. If you start slowly, Buddy will not get the message. He will most likely just sit at heel

and wait for his reward there. But if you start at a fast pace, as if you are running late, his first instinct will be to follow your step.

4. You can either walk in a straight line or a large circle in a clockwise motion.

5. The goal of this exercise is to get Buddy to walk nicely by your left side. However, once he starts walking, you will notice that he is not that interested in walking at heel. When he leaves your side, lock your hands around the leash to apply some tension and return him back to the "*heel*" position. Anytime Buddy tries to get ahead of you, bring him back to your side. His shoulder should be in line with your left hip.

6. Make a couple of steps, then stop, mark the behavior, and lavish him with verbal praises and treats.

7. Repeat this a dozen times, each time adding a couple more steps. It will take a few tries before Buddy can understand what you are trying to achieve. Just make sure to put energy into your walking in order to keep his focus on you. Make it your initial goal to make 10 steps without touching the leash. Once you manage to achieve that, it won't be long before Buddy masters this command completely.

What If Buddy is Very Stubborn?

If your dog is fighting you and you cannot get him to make a couple of steps without him trying to take the lead, then perhaps you should try luring him with treats:

1. Instruct him to "*sit*" on your left side. Attach the leash and place it over your right shoulder, again, allowing about 4 inches of slack. Place some treats in your left hand.

2. Keep your right hand at waist height, and make a tunnel around the leash. Hold the treat hand near Buddy's nose.

3. Give him the "**Heel**" command and start walking at a brisk pace. Keep your hand with the treat in front of Buddy to lure him to take a step forward.

4. Make a couple of steps, then stop, mark the behavior, and give Buddy the treat.

5. Repeat this 5-6 times, each time increasing the distance. Once Buddy becomes comfortable with the maneuver, try this exercise without the treat.

Changing Direction

Congratulations! Your dog can now walk in a straight line (or a circle) calmly by your left side. But are you two ready to make it through a crowded place just yet? Before you fool yourself into thinking you are ready to handle traffic, you need to make sure that Buddy can stay at heel even when making a turn.

Right Turn

In order for your dog to continue walking at heel when you are making a right turn, your ball of fur will need to increase his pace. If you try this now, you will probably end up turning right while Buddy will continue walking in the other direction. At this stage, when your dog is still new to training and is not able to give you a hundred percent, you need to trick him into making a turn as well.

Instruct Buddy to walk at heel. Before you make a right turn, say his name in an upbeat tone. When he looks up at you, make the turn, and continue walking. Hearing his name will cause Buddy to look at you, which will help him notice that you are changing the direction. That way, he can stay with you even when making a right turn.

About-Turn

An about-turn, technically, is making a right turn twice. Which means that you will need to say Buddy's name twice, in order to keep his attention and make sure that he continues walking at heel.

If he has trouble following you, you can lure him into making a turn with a treat. But, since most dogs become overly stimulated by this method, make sure not to use the treat lure unless you absolutely have to.

Left Turn

If you try to make a left turn now, you will probably bump into Buddy. For this turn, Buddy does not need to look at you but to slow down his pace so you can both make a left turn, safely.

But for him to slow down, you have to slow down, first. So, instruct the "*heel*," start walking, and then slow down the pace. Draw back on his leash using your left hand, and then slowly make the left turn. After doing so, return your hand back to its initial position (the funnel around the leash), and resume your faster pace.

Down from a Distance

This is, perhaps, one of the most important commands that you can teach your dog. Once you can command him to drop down on a dime, even from across the street, then you've achieved an incredible control of Buddy's activity.

Okay, but doesn't "*come*" do the same thing? Sure, if you see that your ball of fur is chasing a squirrel and is about to cross a busy street to get it, you can use the "*come*" command to get him to stop. However, when you say "*come*," you are actually asking Buddy to stop, turn around, come back to you and forget all about the squirrel. That's simply a lot to ask. And since your dog is probably super determined to get that squirrel, at such challenging times, the "*come*" command may not even work.

The "*down,*" command, on the other hand, is a lot different. First of all, when you shout "*Down*" from a distance, all you're asking Buddy to do is to simply drop down to the ground. He doesn't even have to move his eyes away from the squirrel. After a couple of seconds, when you get to Buddy, his arousal level will have already decreased, so it will be much easier for him to shift his attention to you.

Here is how you can train Buddy to drop down from a distance:

1. Attach the leash to his collar and stand in front of him, facing him. Hold the leash with one hand and then instruct Buddy to "*sit.*"

2. Now, gently take a step back, and give him the **"Down"** command. Since Buddy has been practicing "*Down*" from Week 1, chances are he is already pretty good at this command by now.

3. When he lays down, immediately mark the behavior and give him a treat.

4. It is super <u>important</u> to add some variety to this training. If you give Buddy the "*down*" command every time you take a step or two backward, he will soon associate the command with your steps, and will most likely begin offering the behavior every time he notices you are about to step away, as he will have learned that making a step backward means "*down*" and reward. To avoid that, keep the exercise unpredictable. Sometimes,

take a step backward, mark the behavior, and then return to Buddy to give him the reward. Or ask Buddy to "*sit*" when you step away.

5. Once Buddy begins offering the "*down*" position easily, start increasing the distance. Instead of making one step, take two steps backward. Then take three, four… Gradually increase the distance until Buddy will have no problem laying down even if you give him the command from across the room.

When you manage that, see how you will do without the leash and without instructing Buddy to "*sit*" first. Practice for as long as it takes for your dog to become comfortable laying down when you tell him to, even if he is on his own time, digging in the backyard or sniffing around in the park off-leash.

What If Buddy Doesn't Want to Lie Down?

Keep in mind that your dog already knows the "*down*" command. He has learned that "*down*" is performed from a sitting position when you are next to him. He is probably just confused because you have decided to change the rules of the "*down*" he is familiar with. Make sure that you are not more than one step away from him, and do not increase the distance before he becomes more comfortable with the new game. Step away, ask for the "*down*" and wait a couple of seconds. If Buddy won't do it even when you are just a step away, then lure him with a treat by lowering it to the ground. Click and reward. Repeat this until your dog can do this without the lure. Then try by taking two steps, then three, and so on.

Stay Longer

Many new owners think that "*stay*" and "*wait*" are the same, so they often use both commands to elicit the same behavior. But that is a huge mistake to make. "*Stay*" is a very different command than the "*wait*" exercise that we covered in the second week. While "*wait*" means "pause," "*stay*" means "hold that position until I tell you otherwise."

You can see how different they are, as well as how confusing using them interchangeably can be for Buddy. For instance, if you are about to leave your house and go to work, you tell your Buddy to "*wait*" in order for him to give you some space to go outside and close the door. You don't tell him to "*stay*," which technically means "do not move from that spot until I get back from work," as that's impossible.

The Three D's

According to most trainers, the *stay* command has three main elements:

#1: **D**uration – how long your dog *stays*

#2: **D**istractions – how capable the dog is to *stay* when distractions are present

#3: **D**istance – how far you will move away from your dog when you ask him to *stay*

These three elements are incredibly important for the training process of this command, and, therefore, it is critical for you to follow the order, meaning that you should work on the duration first, then introduce distractions, and finally, instruct the command from a distance.

Here is how you can teach your Bud to "*stay*" in a certain position:

1. Instruct Buddy to "*sit*." Praise him verbally and then hold up a treat. Wait for a second, then mark the behavior and give him the reward. Make sure to feed Buddy calmly to prevent him from jumping up.

2. Use a release word to encourage your Buddy to get up. Most people choose "Okay" for the release word, but if you are using okay in conversation often, you might choose another one to avoid confusing your dog. *Release, Get Up, Free, Break, At Ease, Done,* etc. are all good examples for a release word. When Buddy gets up, you can give him another treat to reward him for being a good boy, but do not mark the behavior. You are teaching "*stay*" after all, so you should put the emphasis on that command.

3. Repeat the process again, only this time, say **"Stay"** when you show him the treat. Hold the treat up for 2 seconds and make sure to place it either under Buddy's nose or far enough so he will not be able to nibble on it.

4. Mark the behavior and give him the treat. Use the release word to encourage him to get up.

5. Repeat, but this time, try to hold the treat for 3 seconds. Working on the *duration* is very important, so repeat this for as long as it takes for Buddy to be able to maintain that position for ten seconds. Make sure to use the verbal cue all the way through, to remind him that he should "*stay*."

6. Once Buddy is able to *"stay"* for longer than 10 seconds, you can then introduce small distractions. Instruct him to *"stay"* and then take a hop. Immediately mark the behavior, give him the treat, and release. Repeat the *"stay"* again, hop on one foot, wait for a second, then hop on the other foot. Mark, reward, release. Gradually build up the distractions until your Buddy is able to *"stay"* even when you are hopping up and down, clapping your hands, spinning in a circle, etc. Remember to introduce distractions gradually. You want Buddy to succeed in mastering the *"stay."*

7. When your dog is able to remain in the same position for about 20-30 seconds with distractions, you can then start working on the third D – the distance. However, you cannot instruct him to *"stay"* from a distance when there are distractions present. Remove the distractions, take a step away from your dog, and instruct Buddy to *"stay."* Mark, reward, release. The second time, take two steps away. Then three, four, five… Gradually increase the distance, but <u>always return to Buddy to reward him.</u> Do not call your dog to come to you from a distance, as that may motivate him to break the *"stay"* in order to come to you and get the reward.

8. When your dog can *"stay"* even when you are not near him, you can gradually start combining the three D's.

The technique above is for teaching Buddy to *"stay"* from a sitting position. You can also use the same method to teach him to remain in a *"down"* position. Simply, instead of instructing him to *"sit,"* tell Buddy to lie *"down"* before teaching him the *"stay."*

What if Buddy Gets Up Before You Release Him?

If your dog gets up before you give him the release word, then you should include a negative punishment to motivate him to remain in that position in order to get the reward. Just put your hand with the treat behind your back, and say *"Oops,"* to let Buddy know that he has done something wrong. Then, wait a couple of seconds and repeat again. Instruct him to *"sit,"* then hold up the treat where he can see it. He needs to understand that getting up without hearing the release word makes the treat go away. If he gets up again, do it all over. Repeat this for as long as it takes for Buddy to get the message.

Relax!

How many times have you forced yourself to go out or fake a smile and ended up having a good time and genuinely smiling? We often need to be reminded to hit the pause button and just relax. Your Bud has had a pretty intense week. You have been teaching him three challenging commands that soak up a lot of his energy. Even if his constant jumping up and down tells you otherwise, your dog probably craves rest. Sometimes, you should remind him to take a rest after a long day to nurture his mental being and preserve his strength for the following training.

Teaching Buddy to "*relax,*" basically means telling him to go lie down on his side. Besides the fact that this command will help him recharge his batteries, it is also needed for some of the most popular games you can play with your dog.

1. Instruct Buddy to lie down. Once he does that, give him a treat, but do not mark the behavior. Remember, you should put the emphasis on "*relax,*" not "*down.*"

2. Now, take a look at his "*down*" position. In order for you to teach him the "*relax,*" Buddy needs to be lying on his hip, with his hind legs to the side. If that is the case, you can skip this step.

3. If Buddy is not in that position and is in a perfect square, you need to rock him onto his hip. To do so, place a treat in front of Buddy's nose, then move it toward the place between his hip and shoulder, making a semicircle. Buddy will most likely follow the yummy treat with his nose and rock onto his hip on his own. Mark the behavior and give him the treat.

4. Once your dog is on his side, move the treat over the point of his spine, until Buddy begins to roll onto his side. Once he starts doing that and ends up in a "C" curl, move the reward toward his head to the floor, in front of his nose. Now, this is the moment where your dog is supposed to put his head to the floor in order to get the treat. As soon as he does that, say **"Relax,"** then mark the behavior and give Buddy the reward.

5. Repeat luring Buddy into this position, until he becomes really familiar with it and starts offering it easily. Then, you can phase out the lure, and start giving the verbal cue to elicit the behavior.

What If Buddy Is Tense and Won't Relax?

If you are dealing with a tense dog who refuses to turn his head all the way, then you need to shape the behavior. Watch your dog's behavior and notice when he makes the jump up. Most tense dogs just move their heads a few inches and then jump up, refusing to rock onto the hip. If that is the case, you need to increase the turn gradually, inch by inch. Note after how many inches your dog jumps up. If he turns his head 4 inches, then mark his behavior after the third inch and give him a reward. Next time, do it after 4 inches, and so on until he is encouraged to turn all the way.

Week 4 Training

After three weeks of training, your dog is now not only ready to take a nice walk and come to you when called, but he is also able to remain in a certain position until you tell him otherwise, as well as to drop down even when instructed from a distance. That surely makes life with a canine a lot easier and more entertaining. However, you still have a long way to go before you can actually brag to your friends about having a well-mannered ball of fur.

Before you jump to teaching Buddy fun games to show off your training skills, you first need to make sure that he masters a few more important commands:

Take It!

Having a dog that has mastered the skill to retrieve is one of the most important indicators that you have succeeded in training. The *"take it"* command is the starting point for mastering retrieve, and it is also the easiest thing to teach. Since your dog does nothing but *take* things pretty much most of the time, you will have tons of opportunities to capture the desired behavior on a daily basis. But since taking things is something Buddy enjoys, jumping straight to the verbal cue shouldn't be a problem:

1. Start with something that you know Buddy will take, like his favorite doggy treats. Place one in your hand, stand next to Buddy, show him the treat, and say **"Take It."**

2. As he closes his jaw to get the treat, mark the behavior so that he understands that's the desired behavior.

3. Repeat the same process, but make it a bit more challenging by placing the treat someplace where Buddy shouldn't be able to get it as easily. For instance, place the treat

behind you or even better, move your hand away as you offer him the treat so that he will have to follow it. Say **"Take It,"** let him have the treat and mark the behavior.

4. Then, try it with his favorite toy. Make a squeaky sound to get his attention and get him excited. Tease him with the toy a bit before offering it to him. As his mouth closes on it, mark the behavior and give him a reward to encourage him to repeat it. Now, he will probably drop the toy to get his reward, but that's okay. The point is to *"take"* the object when you are offering it, not to hold it.

5. Once he is familiar with taking things from your hand, let him practice this on the floor. Toss his toy in front of you, and as you do it, say **"Take It."** Once he picks it up, mark the behavior, and give him the reward. If your Buddy doesn't want to pick objects off the floor, try to gradually decrease your hand to the floor when you are practicing this command, to get him used to taking things from that height.

6. Gradually increase the distance by tossing the toy further away. It won't be long before you can spend an hour playing fetch in your backyard.

What If Buddy Refuses to Take Things?

No dog will refuse to take yummy treats from your hand (unless he is dealing with some medical issues), that's a fact. But what if your dog takes his favorite toy and treats with ease but is not interested in taking other objects that you are offering him?

If your dog doesn't want to take other things, try to shape the behavior:

1. Instruct Buddy to *"take"* an object. If he refuses, place the object on the floor, or on a chair, and step away. Let him explore it first.

2. Every time he looks at the object, mark the behavior and give him a treat. Once he realizes that the object gives him the reward, he will be encouraged to go near it, and maybe even *"touch"* it with his nose. When he does that, mark and reward. Make sure to stop rewarding Buddy for looking at the object when he starts touching it with his nose.

3. As the touches become more frequent, he will eventually open his mouth to make contact. When that happens, lavish him with treats, give him his favorite toy, play a game, etc. The point is to celebrate the performed behavior to let Buddy know how

positive "*taking*" that object is. Again, once he "*takes it*," stop rewarding him for touching it so that he can get the message.

4. Perform this with other objects as well. Chances are, teaching "*take it*" to Buddy now is a lot easier than it was in the beginning.

Give!

As beneficial teaching "*take it*" can be, trust me, having your dog master "*give*" will have an even greater significance. Since Buddy loves playing the "*take it*" game so much, he will be running around with a valuable and forbidden object in his mouth sooner rather than later. When that happens, begging and pleading with your dog will not do the trick. Bribing him with a piece of sausage may also be risky as he may drop down the object and end up causing damage. Besides, what if you don't have any yummy bribes with you?

For these situations, the "*give*" command is a true lifesaver. "*Giving*" you objects on cue can teach Buddy that not everything you own should be used to play a round of chase-me.

1. Fill your pockets with doggy treats. Take Buddy's favorite toy in one hand. Squeak or shake it to get his attention. Once he gets excited, offer the toy to him or simply drop it on the floor so he can catch it.

2. When he has it in his mouth, grab a treat and show it to him, while saying **"Give."**

3. When Buddy opens his mouth to take the treat, he'll drop the toy on the floor. Mark the behavior. With your other hand, gently take the toy. Let Buddy nibble on the treat, but do not give him the whole thing until you have the toy in your other hand.

4. Once you are holding the toy, show it to Buddy and give him the whole treat.

5. Practice this for as long as it takes for your dog to start "*giving*" you his toys willingly. When that's achieved, you should be able to retrieve a forbidden object just as easily.

What If Buddy Loves Playing with the Toy but Refuses to Give a Forbidden Object?

If your dog has learned the "*give*" command with his toy but when the time comes to really "*give*" a forbidden object, he refuses, it probably is because he already knows that "*giving*" you the object means game over. Do not just take things from him; make sure to spend some time playing the "*give*" game as well. It doesn't matter if Buddy knows what "*give*" means. Continue playing the *"give"* game with his toy (when Buddy actually gets the toy at the end), in order to keep him enthusiastic about the word *"give."* Also, do not forget to lavish him with treats whenever he *"gives"* you a forbidden object.

Caution: *Do NOT practice this command if your dog growls, tenses, or tries to bite when approaching her to get the object. If Buddy shows any signs of aggression, immediately seek help from a qualified trainer or behavior professional.*

Leave It!

Once you start going on longer walks, you will notice that the thing that Buddy loves the most is chewing on stuff he finds in the park. And most of these times, those things will be truly disgusting. That's when telling him to leave stuff alone comes in handy. Being able to tell Buddy to *"leave"* the sharp bone piece he spotted in the gutter can be truly beneficial. Not to mention how useful this command can be when setting up the dinner table or when Buddy gets tempted to steal the pizza slice that your toddler has been nibbling on for hours.

Here is how you can teach a basic, *"leave it"* command:

1. Hold a treat that is not squishable (freeze-dried meat works best) in front of Buddy. Have a few more treats in your other hand, and hold them behind your back.

2. Make sure you have Buddy's attention, and then place the treat under your foot's ball." At the same time, firmly say **"Leave It."** Buddy can sniff and nibble on the treat, but do not let him have it. You should think about wearing shoes that cannot be damaged.

3. The point here is to wait for Buddy to give up and stop licking the treat. When that happens, mark the behavior immediately, and give him the treat.

4. Gradually start increasing the delay between the time Buddy *"leaves"* the treat and the time you mark the behavior so that he can stay away from the yummy piece of liver for longer periods.

5. Repeat this for as long as it takes for Buddy to start *"leaving"* the treat alone when he hears the verbal cue *"Leave It."* When he can manage to resist touching the treat for a few seconds, practice a bit more tempting exercise. This time, try to cover only half of the treat with your foot, leaving half uncovered and free to be nibbled on. If Buddy dives to take the uncovered liver, cover it with your foot quickly, and say **"Oops."** Your dog

needs to understand that reaching for the treat makes the reward go away. Then mark and reward him. Repeat this for as long as it takes for him to be able to resist the temptation and *leave* uncovered treats alone for a few seconds.

What If Buddy Cannot Stop Licking?

You need to be patient. Eventually, Buddy will realize that he cannot reach the treat, and he will just give up. If you think that the licking is taking longer than it's supposed to, then perhaps Buddy can reach the treat from under your foot. See if you can tip the foot to keep him away from the prize. Keep in mind that if he can touch the treat, he is being reinforced and, therefore, will never learn how to "*leave it*" properly.

Leave It When Dropped

Imagine this scenario: You are making a ham sandwich when all of a sudden, your hand slips and the entire container with leftover ham slices drops on the floor. Buddy, who has been sitting beside you the whole time hoping that you will reward him with a slice, doesn't think twice about diving into that container. Will "*Leave It*" work when such a tempting situation occurs? In order to prepare Buddy (and yourself) for these temptations, a good amount of practice is required first. Make sure to exercise the "*Leave It*" game when tasty treats are dropped in order to train Buddy to leave stuff alone even when it's super hard to resist.

1. Instruct Buddy to sit in front of you. With a firm but positive tone, say **"Leave It"** and immediately drop a yummy treat so that it falls on the side and slightly behind you. This is important as you will need to get in front of the treat if Buddy's first instinct is to grab it.

2. Wait for Buddy to look away once he realizes that he cannot reach the sausage piece. When that happens, mark the behavior and let him have the treat.

3. Repeat this and gradually start placing the treat in places where you cannot guard it from him, until Buddy is ready to "*leave it*" on cue, regardless of where you've dropped it.

4. But since in temptation alley the food will be dropped first, you need to turn the exercise around and try to drop the treat first, and then tell Buddy to "*leave it.*" Again, if

necessary, block the treat to prevent Buddy from reaching it. Practice for as long as it takes for Buddy to be able to resist the urge to grab the treat.

What If Buddy Cannot Resist the Temptation When Out for a Walk?

If your dog has already mastered the *"Leave It"* command at home and looks the other way when you tell him not to take the dropped lasagna from the floor, but struggles to pay attention to your commands when someone drops a piece of hot dog in the park, then perhaps you should work on the exercise a bit more:

1. Ask a family member or a friend to help you out. Put Buddy on a leash, allowing a slack of a couple of inches. Give your friend some doggy food that Buddy doesn't particularly love, and position them so that they are about 20 feet away from you.

2. Let your accomplice start walking toward you, dropping treats along the way. Grab Buddy's leash and stroll toward your friend as well. Give Buddy the **"Leave It"** cue and continue walking. Make sure to restrain Buddy so that he cannot reach the treats. Once you are out of the 'danger zone' (the treats' vicinity), mark Buddy's behavior, and give him a tasty treat as a reward.

3. After 2-3 repetitions, let your friend drop tastier treats. Do the same thing and gradually increase the taste of the treats until you have some really irresistible pieces of liver dropped on the floor. The goal is to have Buddy look the other way. Until that happens, keep restraining him to prevent him from reaching for the treats. This is really important as reaching the treat means reinforcing the behavior.

4. Once you are at least 80 percent sure that you don't have to put pressure on the leash and that Buddy will look the other way when you give him the verbal cue, then you can try practicing the same exercise in different locations. Try your backyard, the nearest park, an uncrowded sidewalk, etc. Finally, try this exercise without the leash. If Buddy offers the *"Leave It"* behavior willingly, he is ready for the endless temptations of the outer world.

Go to Your Place

No matter how much you love spending your afternoons with your furry friend, there will be times when you will simply need to hit a pause and break from Buddy's company. Sometimes, your dog will have the same need, as well. Every dog needs to have its own place in the home. Someplace where they can go to sleep, be alone, or just relax after a good meal. A place where you can send Buddy to when you want to have a quiet dinner, or when your old aunt comes to visit.

Method 1

The first method is teaching Buddy how to go to his spot by shaping his behavior. Shaping *"go to your place,"* means allowing your dog to fully engage his brain, which can also be beneficial for other exercises as well.

By shaping, you simply set up the environment to let Buddy perform the behavior, then you mark and reward. It's a fun way to teach and learn:

1. Place a mat (or a rug) on the floor. Have your Buddy nearby and fill your pockets with treats.

2. Watch Buddy's behavior closely. You are simply waiting for him to associate with the placed mat. Every time he looks at the mat, immediately mark the behavior and give him a treat.

3. Once you notice that Buddy is getting closer to the mat, mark immediately and give him the treat, but either throw the treat behind you or place it on the floor near you. The point is for Buddy to get away from the mat and "reset" his movement by returning to you. That way, you can begin the practice from scratch.

4. Eventually, Buddy will catch on and understand that getting closer to the mat gets him rewarded. Once he starts getting closer to the mat easily, try to get him to sit. To tell your dog that you want him to go to his place, you need a verbal cue. *Mat, Place, Spot, Settle,* are all good examples.

5. The point here is to wait for Buddy to sit or lie down on the mat on his own. The instant that happens, say **"Place"** or whatever cue you want to use, mark, and reward. Repeat for as long as it takes for Buddy to associate that cue word with that mat. You can then place the mat in your kitchen, living room, or wherever you want Buddy to settle, and ask your dog to go to his spot and be alone for a while.

Keep in mind that this method takes patience, but it is also more beneficial as this way you allow your dog to engage his mind and learn how to solve problems on his own. If this is too overwhelming for you, or if you don't have the time for shaping, try the luring method below.

Method 2

1. Place the mat on the floor. Call Buddy in the same room and make sure you are both standing about two feet from the mat.

2. Hold a yummy treat in your hand. Show the hand to Buddy and gently lure him to the mat with the treat hand. Say "**Place**" or your preferred verbal cue, at the same time.

3. Once Buddy is standing on the mat, instruct him to "*Sit.*" Mark the behavior and reward him with the treat.

4. Repeat this a few times and make sure to point toward the mat with your treat hand while saying the verbal cue.

5. After a few repetitions, instead of instructing Buddy to sit, use the "*down*" command. Make sure to reward Buddy for staying in his place to help him associate the mat as something positive that gets him rewarded.

6. Once Buddy starts to catch on, use the verbal cue and then wait to see what his reaction will be. If he starts walking toward the mat, mark, and reward. While rewarding him for getting closer to the mat, start moving farther away. This is important as, ultimately, the "*Go to your spot*" command should be instructed from a distance.

Tip: Trick Buddy into falling in love with the mat. Make sure to put treats and all sorts of lovely surprises there for him to find, so he can think of 'his spot' as something positive and rewarding, not a place where he will be lonely.

Dealing with Misbehavior

You have managed to successfully house train your dog and teach him all of the commands from above. Congratulations! You can now take long walks even off-leash, without the fear of Buddy's (or other living species') wellbeing. But even though your Buddy knows the meaning of a lot of your English words, he still has a long way to go before becoming the wonderfully well-mannered pet.

Dogs often show a lot of behavioral problems that are not only bad and annoying, but sometimes dangerous, as well. Here are some of the most common ways in which dogs misbehave and how to prevent them from happening:

Excessive Barking

No one likes having a barker around. Besides the fact that your neighbors are definitely not appreciating Buddy's loud barking, keep in mind that this problematic behavior is also illegal in some places. For the sake of everyone in Buddy's vicinity, you need to come up with a way to put a stop to his excessive barking. But in order to do that, you need to first pinpoint why your dog is barking in the first place. Assuming that you have ruled out the possibility that your dog is dealing with a medical issue or is barking because he needs to go potty, here are the different types of barkers and how to shush them:

Request Barking

Request barking is one of the most common problems that dog owners have. It happens when your dog is seeking your attention and barks in hopes of getting the thing he wants from you.

Do not Reinforce. The first step you need to take to stop your dog from attention barking is to simply stop giving him what he wants. Of course, keep in mind that this cannot happen overnight and that you will probably need some time to teach him that request barking gets him no positive results, especially if he is already used to getting what he wants with each bark.

Ignore His Barking. However, simply stopping the reinforcement will probably not do the trick, or it will take a lot of time for him to understand that he is doing it in vain. Meanwhile, try to ignore his request barking. Keep in mind that in Buddy's mind, even telling him to stop is giving him attention. This will lead to no positive results but will most likely only encourage him to continue barking. When Buddy is barking, simply go about your day. Do not give him a shred of attention. In fact, do not even look at him. Just keep yourself distracted and try not to think too much of how annoying his barking sound is.

Reward the Silence. Here is where positive reinforcement comes in handy. Once your dog stops barking, immediately mark the behavior, either with a clicker, by making a sound that you will use for marking or simply by telling Buddy that he has been a good boy. Then, give him a yummy treat. Do this every time Buddy stops his barking. Over time, your dog will learn that becoming silent gives him rewards, which will motivate him to stop barking.

Once he catches on, you need to work on delaying the rewards, otherwise, Buddy will play a bark-and-stop game in order to get treated as often as possible. Do the exercise from above for a couple of days. The third day, when Buddy stops barking, wait a couple of seconds before giving him the treat. Wait for 5 seconds, then 10, and work your way up until Buddy waits for a minute or two in silence before getting the reward.

Tip: Vary the length of time between the moment your dog stops barking, and when you give him the treat. That way, Buddy will not become used to getting rewards and will not come to expect a piece of sausage after a certain amount of time.

Find an Alternative Behavior. I agree that replacing his attention-seeking desires with training lessons or other exercises may be time-consuming and somewhat overwhelming, but there is no doubt that this is the best way to teach your dog if he wants your attention, he has to engage in other activities. That creates an amazing opportunity for you to teach Buddy desirable behavior, whether it is a new command you have been working on or a fun game to pass the time. So, instead of responding to his requests, instruct Buddy to sit and teach him something else while you have his undivided attention.

Alarm Barking

It is nice to have your dog give you a heads-up when there is someone at the door. But if Buddy perceives everyone passing near your house to be an intruder and starts barking loudly for hours, now that is surely a problem.

You can easily recognize alarm barking. With each bark, the dog alarm barking pounces forward or makes a slight lunge.

The "Quiet" Command

Believe it or not, you can actually teach your dog to stop barking excessively on cue. It doesn't matter how territorial Buddy is; if you are consistent about the training routine and patient enough to let your dog succeed, you will soon teach him to stop barking on cue, just like you instruct him to sit down.

1. Once you notice that your dog is alarm barking, grab a treat and show it to him. This should be enough for him to get distracted and shift his attention to you.

2. Wait until your dog stops barking. The second he stops, firmly say

3. **"Quiet."** Then, immediately mark the behavior and give Buddy the treat.

4. Repeat this every time you notice your dog guarding his territory and barking at perceived intruders. After a dozen repetitions or so, you can start giving him the verbal cue *"quiet"* before he stops barking to elicit the behavior. Of course, that means that you also shouldn't be showing him the treat anymore, but wait for him to earn it. If Buddy complies, mark the behavior and give him the treat. If not, then you probably need to lure him with the treat some more. Eventually, he will learn to do it without the freeze-dried liver.

5. Now that you think your dog can actually stop barking on cue, it is time to apply this command and test his behavior. Have a friend slam the car door upfront or make a noise in front of your house. Wait for Buddy's reaction with a treat in your hand. If Buddy starts barking, say **"Quiet,"** but do not show him the treat. If he stops, mark the behavior and reward him. If not, then you probably need to spend some more time training.

Discouraging Jumping Up

All dogs love jumping up. And to be honest, most of us like that too. Except when the dog is covered in mud or when he is about to knock down your 95-year-old uncle. But it is in their nature to jump. In fact, when we pick them up as puppies and cuddle them near our chest, we actually reinforce the jumping behavior. If that is not as cute as it was when Buddy was a cuddly ball of fur and you want to discourage this behavior, you first have to get everybody on board and make sure that none of you will encourage the behavior by rewarding it with patting and smooches.

Below you will find an on-leash and off-leash exercise that you need to perform with Buddy in order to train him not to jump up on you, as well as a tried-and-true technique to stop Buddy from greeting visitors too enthusiastically.

The On-Leash Exercise

1. Have a friend or a family member help you out with this exercise. Give him a treat and ask him to start approaching you and Buddy. Call Buddy and attach the leash to his collar.

2. Hold Buddy's leash and make sure to stand still. Tell your friend to start approaching you and to hold the treat up against his chest.

3. Do not allow leash slack so Buddy cannot get up. Once he notices that he cannot jump up to your helper to get the treat, he will eventually get frustrated and sit down. The instant he does that, mark the behavior, and let your friend give him the treat.

4. Repeat this process about a dozen times. It usually takes dogs about 5-6 repetitions to figure out that sitting down when being approached is what gets them rewarded. If your dog needs more training to catch on, don't worry. Keep repeating until Buddy starts to sit down willingly.

5. After a dozen repetitions, try again, but this time, offer a few inches of slack. Let your friend approach you with the treat up against his chest. Wait for Buddy's reaction. If his first instinct is to sit down, then he has already learned the point. Mark the behavior and give him the treat immediately. If he jumps up to get the treat, have your friend whisk out the reward and firmly say **"Oops."**

6. Once Buddy sits down again, mark the behavior, and give him the treat.

When you don't have a friend to help you out, you can try this on your own. Simply, attach Buddy's leash to something, allowing a little slack. Stand about 10 feet away from him and wait for Buddy to sit down. Start approaching him. As long as he is sitting down, keep approaching until you get close to him to mark and reward. The instant Buddy jumps up, stop, say **"Oops"** and whisk out the treat. Eventually, he will learn that sitting calmly gets him rewarded.

The Off-Leash Exercise

But what about those times when you walk through the door and Buddy greets you in an overly excited, almost brutal way? There is surely no way to leash restrain him there. When that happens, the best tactic is to simply *ignore* him.

1. Keep a jar with doggy treats in the entryway or have biscuits with you all the time. Walk through the door and see what Buddy's reaction is.

2. If he starts jumping up, simply look away and avoid eye contact. From the corner of your eye, watch Buddy's movements and when he is about to jump up on you, step away from him.

3. Wait for Buddy to get frustrated for not getting his attention and sit down. The instant he does that, mark the behavior with a clicker, a kissing sound, or by telling him that he is a good boy. Then, give him the reward.

4. Keep repeating this every time you walk through the front door until Buddy realizes that sitting down gets him rewarded.

Jumping Up on Guests

The on-leash and off-leash exercises are great for teaching your Buddy to give you some space when you come home from work. But will they work when you have your sister and her toddlers come for a visit? I don't think so.

This is how you can get Buddy to keep 'all four on the floor' when you have visitors:

1. There are a couple of ways you can train Buddy not to jump up at the door. However, by far the most successful one is if you provide a special place for him to sit and greet the guests in a calm manner. A normal-sized mat placed in your entryway will serve the purpose well. The first thing you need to do is, of course, get Buddy to sit and lie down on it so he can get familiar.

2. Place a treat on the mat and get Buddy to come to the entryway. When he notices the treat and comes closer to the mat to eat it, say **"Mat."**

3. Stand a couple of feet away, point to the mat, and say the verbal cue again. Your dog will probably be confused so you might need to throw a treat onto the mat for him to get the idea.

4. Then, after your dog eats the treat, get closer and show him another treat. If he jumps up, whisk the treat away and say **"Oops."** Then, point to the mat and say **"Mat"** again. Wait for Buddy to sit on the mat then mark the behavior and immediately give him the treat.

5. Repeat this for as long as it takes for Buddy to learn that *"Mat"* means *go sit on the mat and wait for your reward there*. Once he starts offering the behavior easily, you can then combine it with a *stay* command to train him to spend some more time on the mat.

6. Then, enlist help from a family member or a friend. Let them knock on the door. When Buddy gets too excited, say **"Mat"** and wait for him to sit there before opening the door. Once you open the door, say **"Stay"** and toss Buddy a treat. Keep repeating until he understands that he should stay on the mat until the guests have taken off their shoes and coats and are inside the house. Do not forget to praise and reward to encourage the behavior, though.

No Begging, Please

There is nothing more annoying than, when there are friends over for dinner, to have your Bud sitting on the floor, touching every guest with his furry paws, whining and begging to get a slice of that pot roast that smells heavenly. And while that may seem irresistibly cute at first, having your furry friend disrupt your guests after each bite can easily become annoying and may even ruin what was supposed to be a festive meal.

But don't worry. Teaching your dog good table manners is indeed possible. It may take you a while especially if Buddy has been sweeping crumbs from the dinner table for years, but with a good and consistent routine, you can teach your dog to allow you to have your dinner in peace in just a couple of weeks.

Trying the Cold Shoulder

This method is pretty much letting your dog figure out that he is not wanted at the table, on his own:

1. Get everybody on board. Let all of your family members know that they are not supposed to give Buddy food while you are eating, under no circumstances. And this does not only apply to a nice meal at the dining table. You should not feed Buddy even when having a breakfast cereal in the kitchen, or a quick snack on the couch when watching your favorite show.

2. Avoid eye contact, at all costs. When Buddy comes begging for food, simply look away and ignore him completely. By looking at him, you are giving him attention, which in his language means *stay here and whine until I give you a bite of this sandwich.*

3. If he starts begging loudly, say **"Oops."** Then go about your dinner. The point is for him to get the message that he should be excluded from family meals.

4. Don't engage and be patient. Your dog will eventually learn that begging at the table leads to no rewards. Give him a chew toy instead and see if he will be patient. If he doesn't make a fuss about not being allowed to even sweep the morsels, make sure to give him a giant reward once you finish dinner. This will encourage him to give you your space and wait patiently for his reward.

If the cold shoulder method is taking too long and yields no results, send Buddy to his spot. Just remember, this can contribute to Buddy associating his *spot* with something negative (being excluded from the dinner) if he is overly sensitive. For most dogs though, this works well. Remind Buddy to stay in his spot throughout the dinner. Once you are finished, give him a giant reward. This is really important: give rewards only AFTER you have finished your meal. Otherwise, your dog will probably make the connection that 'begging' leads to '*go to spot*' which leads to 'getting a reward,' which will probably sound like a pretty good deal to him and motivate him to beg some more.

Stop Licking Me... Or Yourself

Licking is one of the most natural behaviors that dogs have. When they are young puppies, their mother licks their skin to show them love, encourage movement, as well as to keep their bodies clean.

They actually explore the world through their tongue, so licking is something they are born to do. But when the licking becomes excessive, it can not only be annoying to watch (as well as hear) but also pretty embarrassing when you are around other people. If Buddy has developed this bad habit, here is how you can put a stop to it:

Tongue Greeting

If Buddy is used to licking your face when he is greeting you, it is because, to him, that is the most natural way to tell you hello. Besides, the human skin is soft which provides comfort for him. Not to mention that it can be salty, which dogs surely find yummy. If that is annoying you (and other people as well), here is how you can get Buddy to forget this bad habit:

1. When you come home from work, if the first thing that Buddy usually does is lick your face, be prepared. Greet him, but just before he is about to stick his tongue out, turn your face away to discourage this habit.

2. The second he retrieves his tongue and withdraws it from your face, mark the behavior, and give him a giant reward to encourage not licking.

3. Repeat this any time he tries to lick greet you. Once Buddy pulls his tongue away, mark, and reward. Eventually, he will get the idea.

What If Buddy Doesn't Give Up?

If Buddy is very persistent and simply doesn't want to pull his tongue away until it touches your skin, you may need to offer him an alternative. See if you can distract him.

1. Turn your face away just like before. If he doesn't seem to give up, use the "*Sit*" command to distract him.

2. Once he sits, tell him that he has been a good boy and give him a reward.

3. Repeat this for as long as it takes for Buddy to get used to having an alternative greeting with you and welcome you calmly, patiently, and with his tongue in his mouth.

Licking His Body

If your dog is licking himself excessively, that can be pretty annoying to watch, as well as hear. Dogs lick their paws to groom and keep them clean, but mostly because it provides them comfort. But, before you start distracting him so he can forget about this annoying habit, it is recommended that you let his vet check him first to rule out underlying conditions. Dogs are known to be wound healers since their saliva speeds up the healing process, so make sure that your Bud is not dealing with a paw injury you are not aware of. If that is not the reason for the excessive licking and is purely a bad habit, then a good distraction technique is in order:

1. Once you notice Buddy is incessantly licking his skin, immediately offer him a proper chew toy or another safe object that will distract him from licking his paws and keep his mind busy.

2. The moment he accepts the toy and starts chewing on it, mark the behavior, and give Buddy a reward.

3. Repeat this for as long as it takes (it might take a while, be patient) for him to associate the excessive licking with chewing on the toy and getting rewarded. He will try to knock down this habit and chew on toys instead, in hopes of getting the treats.

Keep in mind: You cannot replace licking with chewing on toys. Licking is a natural behavior that you cannot (and shouldn't try to) shake your dog out of. Make sure to offer chew toys only when Buddy is licking his skin <u>excessively</u>. Otherwise, it is okay for him to lick.

Stopping Submissive Wetting

Dogs urinate submissively as a way to appease a potential threat. It is an assertive approach of another member of the group who has a much higher rank. This is a mechanism that helps them survive in the dog pack. But what to do when that high-ranking member is you (or another member in your family)? What if your dog is peeing submissively when you enter through the door because he perceives you as a potential threat -someone Buddy feels the need to submit to in such a way?

In order for you to stop submissive urinating, you have to boost Buddy's confidence, as well as keep things low-key:

Boosting His Confidence

Working on building Buddy's confidence, actually means working on stopping the submissive urinating. How? Because in order for Buddy to stop peeing submissively, he first needs to stop perceiving you as a threat. Once Buddy is confident enough to understand that there is no need to feel threatened in any way, the issue will quickly be resolved.

Reward. Keep rewarding your dog whenever he does something right. This is not only important so that Buddy can learn new commands easily, but also because the feeling of getting something right will make him feel more confident in his capabilities.

Distract. When you know that there will be guests coming home, keep Buddy distracted when they arrive. Play a game of fetch or give him some alternative action to perform so that he can act more appropriately around them. Once the surprise moment has passed, and the guests are inside, he will no longer feel the need to urinate submissively. Do this every time to help Buddy act more confidently around new faces.

Give Him a Goal. At the heart of submissive wetting is a pet that simply wants to please his owner. You need to make sure that Buddy has a goal to achieve for most of the day so that he will not feel the need to urinate as much around you. Maintaining a regular training routine, chewing on toys, going on longer walks, and just keeping him active, will help you achieve that.

Avoiding Drama

Submissive urinating is really not hard to solve. All you need to do to grow Buddy out of this habit is to keep greeting low key and avoid the departure-arrival drama:

1. When you enter through the door, do not pay any attention to Buddy. Do NOT approach him by any means, give him time and let him come to you instead.

2. Greet him without making eye contact. Instead, offer him your palm. This is really important as the palm of your hand transmits only positive energy, while the back of the hand is associated with negative behavior.

3. Let Buddy sniff your hand and do not say a word.

4. Then, pat him under his chin, <u>never</u> on top of the head as that only encourages submissive behavior.

5. Do not reach for your dog and never grab him until he stops being submissive, that is.

6. Keep everyone informed. When you have guests coming over, let them know about your issue and tell them to ignore Buddy as well. Your submissive dog should be given the time to get comfortable on his own. Tell your guests to avoid making eye contact and to let Buddy come to them.

7. Follow these steps for as long as it takes for Buddy to stop wetting submissively around people.

NEVER punish your dog for urinating submissively. Do not yell at him, and by all means, do not get angry. That will only have a counter effect. If your dog notices that you are angry, he will be encouraged to urinate some more. If that makes you even angrier, then Buddy will pee some more. As long as you show anger and dissatisfaction, your dog will get more and more submissive as his response will be to desperately try to turn off that anger.

Fun Games for Practice and Bonding

If you know someone who has a well-trained dog, then chances are, they've already managed to impress you with a trick or two. And while it may seem that teaching your dog these fun games is almost impossible, the truth is, most dogs master them even quicker than other commands. That is because the dog is already trained and has adopted proper habits. So if you were thinking about skipping this chapter because, in your opinion, Buddy couldn't possibly master them, let me convince you otherwise.

The key to teaching these games and tricks is in the *sequencing*. That means that, when trying to teach a new trick to your dog, you need to break it into small components that will be easy for him to master, which will, of course, add up to him learning the whole trick.

Now, get ready to wow your friends and family with these astonishing tricks and games you can play with Buddy:

High-Five

High-Five is probably the most popular trick that you can teach your dog. The goal here is, obviously, to get Buddy to raise one of his paws as high as possible. That can be taught in four sequences:

Sequence 1

1. Sit on the floor and have Buddy in front of you.

2. Make sure to reduce your posture either by squatting in front of Buddy or by kneeling, so that you can ensure that you are not hovering or even leaning over your dog.

3. Place your palm somewhere in the mid-chest area, offer it to Buddy, and say **"Shake,"** or whatever verbal cue you wish to use.

4. Lift his dominant front leg off the floor a couple of inches by taking it with your other hand.

5. Then, slide your hand that you offered to him, down to his paw and give Buddy a gentle shake. As you start shaking his hand, praise him enthusiastically to show him how positive and exciting it is to shake hands.

6. Then, give your dog a treat as a reward and give him the release cue.

7. Do five repetitions over three sessions to help Buddy learn the *shake hands* command.

Sequence 2

1. Sit in front of your dog and, again, reduce your posture to make sure you're not leaning or hovering over him.

2. Offer your palm and give him the *Shake* command. Wait for Buddy's response. If he is not willingly offering this behavior, touch his elbow to remind him what he has to do, and then offer the palm again. Make sure to give Buddy a chance to lift the paw on his own.

3. Once he lifts his paw, take it, then praise, reward, and release.

4. If Buddy is not giving his paw on command, then take it yourself, but praise and reward again.

5. Repeat this for as long as it takes for him to start lifting it on cue.

Sequence 3

1. Just like before, sit in front of Buddy and reduce the posture of your body.

2. Offer him your palm and give the "*Shake*" command. At this point, Buddy should put the paw in your palm, willingly.

3. Praise, reward, and release.

4. If he is not giving you his paw, then you are probably moving too fast. Go back to Sequence 2 and repeat some more.

Sequence 4

1. Sit in front of Buddy with a reduced posture.

2. Offer him the palm and give the "*Shake*" command. Your dog should willingly put the paw into your palm. If not, go back to Sequence 3 and repeat some more.

3. Now, raise your palm as high as your dog can possibly place it. Try doing it in 2-inch increments. Do this about a dozen times, and you will notice how your dog will stretch his paw willingly, each time.

4. Do not forget to praise, reward, and then release.

Roll Over

Just like high-five, rollover is also one of the most popular tricks for the whole family to play with their furry member. For this trick, your dog needs to lie on the floor and then roll over sideways. Of course, Buddy needs to have mastered the *down* command first. If your dog has managed to learn that and responds well to treats, then you will have no problem in helping him master this trick as well.

1. Instruct Buddy to get into the *Down position*.

2. Kneel down in front of your dog, making sure that you are not leaning over him.

3. Have an irresistible treat in your hand and hold it in a way that Buddy will have to look at it over his shoulders.

4. Say **"Roll Over"** and immediately make a gentle circle with the treat hand over his head, making sure that you keep the treat close to his nose the whole time.

5. With the other hand, physically get your dog started in making the *roll* by gently pushing him in the direction that you want him to go.

6. Once your dog has rolled over completely, immediately praise and reward him. Repeat for as long as it takes for Buddy to become relaxed when you are rolling him over.

Sequence 2

1. Instruct Buddy to *lie down* and kneel in front of him.

2. Have a tasty treat in your hand.

3. Say **"Roll Over"** and make a circle with the treat head over his nose. This time, do not help Buddy to roll over with your other hand.

4. If Buddy Rolls over on his own, praise and reward immediately. If not, go back to Sequence 1 and practice some more.

5. Repeat until Buddy is really comfortable and performs the behavior with minimum guidance.

Sequence 3

1. Get Buddy to *lie down* and sit in front of him.

2. Say **"Roll Over"** but this time, do not show him the treat.

3. If Buddy rolls over on cue, your job is almost done. Just practice this some more, until he becomes more relaxed in his position. If not, go back to the previous sequence.

4. Do not forget to praise and reward.

Tug

Who doesn't like to have a well-behaved dog they can play *tug* with? And while you may have heard stories that playing *tug* increases the chances for your dog to show aggressive and dominant behavior, that is simply not true. Playing *tug* with your dog can be quite beneficial actually, as it teaches him to defer to you as well as training him to channel his urges better and to control himself.

Buy a knotted rope for this purpose, and follow these steps:

1. Bring out the rope and play with it for a while. Throw it, shake it, do whatever it takes for it to get Buddy excited.

2. Once Buddy approaches you and grabs it, pull gently on the rope to motivate him to show resistance.

3. Once he does that, say **"Good Boy," and tug.**

4. Then, get even more energetic with the tugging.

5. After about 10 seconds, stop, and give your dog the *Give* command.

6. Once he lets go of the rope, mark the good behavior and then reward.

7. If Buddy refuses to give you the rope, trick him by placing a yummy treat on the floor. Then take the rope away from him.

8. Then, try the *tug* game again. Repeat until you get Buddy to *give* you the rope.

Remember that you should be the one who will win most of the times. However, it is okay to let Buddy win occasionally. Just make sure that, after you are done playing, you put the rope away, as Buddy needs to know that the knotted rope is for playing *tug* only.

Play Dead

This trick is a real crowd-pleaser. It consists of you holding an invisible gun and giving Buddy a *Bang!* So he can roll on his side and play dead. Sounds like too good to pass on? Follow these steps and teach Buddy this super fun trick:

Sequence 1

1. Get Buddy in a *"Down"* position. Hold a treat in your 'gun' hand.

2. Then, lean over your dog, and say **"Bang"** in a firm voice, while pointing your index finger at Buddy. Here, Buddy is supposed to roll on his back or his side.

3. If he does that, mark the behavior and the reward him like crazy. If not, then you should use the treat as you did for the *"Roll Over"* trick to get him to roll on his side.

4. Praise, reward, and then release.

5. Repeat for as long as it takes for Buddy to starts reacting on the *"Bang"* command.

Sequence 2

1. The goal here is to get Buddy to play dead even from a standing or sitting position, without instructing him to get *"down"* first. To do so, get your dog's attention first.

2. Then, lean over him and give him the *"Bang"* command as you point the finger at him. If Buddy is a quick learner, he will lie down, roll over, and play dead. If that happens, mark the behavior immediately, then reward, and release.

3. If he doesn't get what you are asking him to do, put him in the "*down*" position physically, and then trick him to roll over, to show him what you mean. Again, mark, reward, and release.

Sequence 3

1. Now, let's try doing it at a distance. Stand about 2 feet from Buddy, and get his attention.

2. Use the "*Bang*" command and 'shoot' him with your index finger.

3. If Buddy responds, praise, reward, release. If not, show him what is asked of him and start over.

4. Once Buddy gets the point, start increasing the distance gradually until you are 6 feet apart from each other.

Belly Crawl

Another fun game is to get Buddy to crawl on his belly. To do so, perform the following steps:

1. Stand in front of your dog and get him in the "*Down*" position.

2. Hold a treat in front of his nose, but make sure that he cannot grab it.

3. With the treat about 1-2 inches off the ground, slowly make a step back, and very carefully and slowly, move the treat toward you.

4. The point here is for Buddy to start dragging his body forward in order to follow the treat.

5. Once you notice your dog doing that, mark the behavior instantly, and give him the treat.

6. Keep repeating this exercise, allowing Buddy to crawl further and further forward.

7. Once Buddy is comfortable with the exercise, you can fade out the treat and do this in either a hand motion or by teaching a *Crawl* verbal cue. Just say **"Crawl"** every time Buddy starts dragging himself to follow the treat, and he will quickly associate the cue with the dragging behavior.

Take a Bow

Wouldn't it be nice if your dog could *"take a bow"* after performing some of the previous tricks for a friend of yours? Now that would be a real cherry on the top of the cake, wouldn't it? Fortunately, teaching Buddy to take a bow is no more complicated than the previous games. Just make sure that he has already mastered the *"Stand"* and *"Down"* command, and you are good to go:

Sequence 1

1. Get Buddy to stand near you, at a *Heel* position.
2. Place your left palm under Buddy's belly and against the hind legs, apply slight backward pressure.
3. Slide your right hand through his collar and place it under the chin.
4. Then, say **"Take a Bow"** while applying a slight downward pressure there.
5. The point here is for Buddy to be standing on his rear end and lower the front. If he struggles to perform this, see if you can lower his front end with the use of a treat lure.
6. Once he succeeds, mark, reward, and release.
7. Repeat for as long as it takes for him to become comfortable in doing this on his own.

Sequence 2

1. Instruct Buddy to get into a *"Stand"* position. Make sure to keep your left hand under the belly.
2. Say **"Take a Bow"** and gently pat the ground with your other hand, to encourage him.
3. Once he lowers the front end, mark the behavior immediately and give him a reward. Release.

Sequence 3

1. Now, it is time for Buddy to do it on cue. Instruct him to get in a *"Stand"* position.
2. Point to the ground with your right hand, and say **"Take a Bow."**

3. When he does as asked, praise, reward, and release. If he wants to get "*down*," you can use your left hand to gently prop up the rear end.

4. Repeat this for as long as it takes for Buddy to be able to do it on command, without you propping the rear end.

5. When he finally gets the point and takes a bow, give him the "*Stay*" command to hold that position. After a couple of seconds, release.

6. Make sure to praise, and reward, and be ready for some applause.

Phasing Out the Treats

Now that you have instilled discipline and managed to teach good manners and basic commands to your furry friend, you probably wonder how much longer you will be dependent on the stinky treats.

You have been using yummy doggy treats in two ways:

1) To lure your dog into performing a behavior that he otherwise doesn't want to or doesn't know how to perform.

2) To reward your Bud after he has willingly responded in a positive way to your command.

And as much as the treats seem like the most useful training tool (which is in most cases true), they provide your dog with neither relevant nor valuable life rewards. Once you start integrating consistent training into Buddy's life, you will need to start phasing out the treats progressively.

The Food Lures

The first stages of training are comprised of the substitution of the food lures with hand signals and verbal commands. The goal of each command is to use the verbal cue as a lure for your dog to perform the desired behavior.

If Buddy is stubborn and you are still quite dependent on using treats to get his body in a certain position, then the first step you need to do is to replace the food lures with *hand signals*.

In order for you to use the hand signals right, Buddy shouldn't be distracted. So hide the stinky treats in your pockets, and with an empty hand, try to show him what you want him to do. For instance, if you are struggling to get Buddy to sit down and you previously used a treat to get him into a sitting position, you can now do the same thing, only with an empty hand. Your Bud has been following the movement of your hand for so long, that he will probably continue doing so even if you are not holding a treat. Give this a try. If Buddy sits down, mark the behavior, and give him a treat as a reward.

You can also practice this around <u>dinner time.</u> Prepare Buddy's dinner and place his food bowl on the counter. Then give Buddy the verbal command and hand signal for "*Sit.*" If he complies, give him a piece of kibble. If not, take the bowl away. It is pretty simple really: sit and have dinner or refuse to sit down and don't get your bowl. That way, Buddy will be given a chance to catch on quickly, which you can later use for all commands.

The Food Rewards

Eventually, you will want to fade out the food rewards as giving him a piece of sausage every time he sits down is not only inconvenient but will also cause treat dependency. There are a couple of ways or different stages when it comes to phasing out the treat rewards:

Longer Sequences

Whereas a treat at the beginning of the training is definitely needed when your dog manages to lie down, surely it is unnecessary for each subsequent session? Besides, it can also be ineffective as you want your Bud to improve during following training sessions, not to make a huge deal for performing the simplest command that he has already known for a couple of weeks. Look at it this way – you would applaud a 5-year-old for learning how to spell his name, but you surely wouldn't think that a 15-year old deserves a reward for performing the same action.

Once you are sure that your dog knows how to perform a certain behavior, the next time, ask him for a little extra in order to earn the reward. As Buddy's training progresses, increase the length of the sequences for a single reward.

Delay the Reward

In addition, you should also increase the length of the time it takes you to give Buddy the reward after performing the desired behavior. Don't be so quick to fill his mouth with irresistible freeze-dried liver just because he has been a good boy. If you are sure that Buddy has already mastered a particular command, prolong the treat. Keep in mind that the longer you delay giving Buddy the food reward, the more focused he will be on you.

After delaying the reward, you can try asking for several responses for a single reward. In this case, obviously, you should plan to give the reward after the performance of the trickier, more complex behavior.

Other Rewards

Once Buddy can perform several responses for a single reward, it is time to say farewell to the food reward, completely. Think of replacing the yummy treats with fun games, petting, a nice walk, or simply by rewarding him with something else he likes to do.

Phasing out the rewards is extremely important because, after a while, your dog may even stop responding to them. Food rewards are great in the initial stages of training, but in real life, they may be overshadowed by other more interesting things. No dog would choose to sit down and get a reward when he can run and play with other canine companions in the park. The latter seems much more fun, don't you think? That is why the best way to maintain good behavior is to replace the food rewards with some things your dog enjoys more.

Addressing Anxiety Correctly

Dogs are social animals. It is in their genes to have relationships with other dogs from their pack. And that's what we love most about dogs – the fact that we can create a strong social bond with them. After all, that's why we call them man's best friend.

But as much as they love spending time with us, their emotions are even more intense when, all of a sudden, they are found alone in the house. This condition is called *separation anxiety*. It is the emotional response to being separated from the human (or humans) that the dog is attached to the most.

Unfortunately, this condition is not uncommon and is particularly present among rescue dogs. But even though pretty much everyone is aware of it, dog owners usually make the situation worse. How? In hopes to somehow make the dog feel better, they make a big fuss about their departure, which only leaves Buddy feeling more alone. When separation anxiety strikes, it is really important to address it the right way if you want to improve Buddy's emotional health.

Recognize It On Time

Although the root cause is the same, no dog goes through separation anxiety the same way. This emotional condition can take various forms and affect your furry friend with different intensities. Recognizing this condition in Buddy can not only help you address it the right way and improve his mental wellbeing, but it will also contribute to more successful training results, as well.

Here are some of the signs that indicate that your dog is suffering from separation anxiety:

- Follows you around the house when you leave the room, regardless of how briefly you are gone

- When you get ready to leave the house, Buddy is whining, shaking, crying, or panting

- Chewing objects around the house when left alone

- Eliminating waste inside the house when left alone

- Scratching the doors and walls and digging at the floor when left alone

- Neighbors complain about loud and constant barking when you are not at home

Counter Condition It

In theory, counter conditioning a dog means training him to start associating something that he is afraid of with a reward. When the dog is suffering from separation anxiety, the fearful thing here is being separated from your or another family member. To counter condition it, you will have to provide something rewarding in return. Buddy has to associate your departure with something that he really enjoys. And what are the things that dogs love most (besides spending time with you)? Food and toys, of course.

For counter conditioning, think of giving your dog a toy stuffed with yummy treats. Just before you leave the house, give your dog a puzzle toy stuffed with crunchy biscuits, pieces of sausage, freeze-dried liver, and other yummy doggy treats. Another great thing is to also spread the inside of the puzzle with some low-fat peanut butter to keep Buddy busy longer. The goal here is to keep Buddy busy for at least half an hour, which should be enough for him to forget the fact that he was afraid of being left alone.

When you get back home, remove the puzzle toy, and keep it out of his sight. The whole point is for Buddy to be conditioned to being able to have it only when you are not at home.

Make sure not to give Buddy the puzzle toy at other times in order for it to be rewarding. If Buddy is given access to it on other occasions as well, it might not be enough to compensate for the sad feeling when you leave the house.

Desensitize Buddy to Solitude

Keep in mind that there isn't a quick cure that can help your Bud grow out of separation anxiety. If his condition is mild to severe, be realistic and do not expect him to get cured overnight. Another way that can help your dog to knock down the intensity of this condition, is to gradually get him used to being left alone. And the best way to do that is to desensitize him to solitude and help him understand that the fact that you are leaving the house does not equal abandonment.

Keep in mind that this is a process that will most likely take a few weeks, and requires a great deal of patience and consistency. However, it has proven to be super effective and can have positive results in the long haul.

1. The first thing you need to do is to actually work on Buddy's feelings associated with your pre-departure. It is recommended that you gradually get him used to these actions. This is best achieved if you engage in these actions throughout the day without actually leaving the house so that your dog can start perceiving them as less scary. For instance, put on your coat and shoes and walk around your home for some time, then take them off. Take the car keys and jiggle them a couple of minutes, then put them back. Do the same things you do before you leave for work, without actually leaving the house.

2. Work on getting Buddy more used to having you out of his sight by spending more time in another room. Doing this every day should eventually make him feel less alone when you actually leave the house.

3. Once he becomes comfortable with you being out of his sight, try blocking his access to you, for instance, by closing the door. Gradually increase the time your dog spends without having access to you. Just make sure that these out-of-sight stays are in the bathroom or in another room, and not actually out of the house, as this may be too stressful for him at this moment.

4. Do this practice for at least 2-3 weeks before actually going out the door. However, if you have an alternate door you can use, such as a back door, or a garage door, that would be much better. Stay there for a minute or two, then 5, then 10, and gradually increase the amount of time you are out.

5. As you begin increasing the time, you should also start incorporating the puzzle toy here, in order to keep Buddy busy.

Be Patient

Keep in mind that it will take a long time before your dog becomes comfortable with the prolonged time alone. For most dogs, the undesirable and destructive behavior kicks in the first 30-40 minutes after the departure. However, it can take a while before you can actually leave Buddy alone for 40 minutes, comfortably.

Once you manage to leave your dog alone for 60 to 90 minutes, then Buddy is surely able to handle 4-6 hours of solitude. But, even then, see if you can leave him alone for shorter periods of time. If you have a friend or a neighbor that can help you out with this, it can make a huge difference as most dogs are anxious when left completely alone, not when their owner is out of their sight.

Don't Be Afraid to Seek Assistance

If you have tried everything in your power to make Buddy comfortable with being left alone, from crate training to counter conditioning and desensitizing, and yet, he is still shaking when you get ready to leave the house and cannot bear being left alone, then it is probably time to seek help from a CPDT (Certified Professional Dog Trainer). Ask your vet to recommend one to you, or search the internet and find one in your area. A CPDT will surely be able to help you solve the issue and address your dog's condition in a more personalized manner.

Bonus Chapter: Agility Training

Agility training is a competitive but extremely fun doggy sport. The agility course is obstacle-made, and it consists of jumps, walkways, tunnels, and all sorts of interesting things that dogs really love. But, besides doing it for fun or competition, agility training your dog will strengthen your bond, and most importantly, keep him fit, healthy, and in perfect shape.

Because the whole point of the sport is trying to overcome the obstacles mostly by jumping, it is not recommended for young dogs and puppies. The best time for you to introduce agility training to Buddy is between the first and second year of his life.

There are a lot of fun agility training methods and techniques that you can teach Buddy. Here are the best ones to start with in order to help your Bud fall in love with this fun sport:

Tunnels

Tunnels are probably the easiest obstacle to teach, so it is recommended to introduce them first. However, don't go in over your head. Keep in mind that you are teaching Buddy something new; something that probably looks scary to him. You cannot expect him to go through super long tunnels. Start with a short tunnel where Buddy can see through to the other side. Have a friend stand on the other side of the tunnel, waiting for him with his favorite toy. You can even coax him to get inside by placing a couple of yummy treats inside.

Don't forget to praise and reward Buddy when he finally makes it through. Once he becomes more comfortable, you can introduce longer or even curved tunnels.

Contact Obstacles

Contact obstacles are obstacles that have specific ends that Buddy will have to touch with his paws. There are a few contact obstacles that you have to try:

The Dog Walk – Which is a balance beam that has ramps on each end.

The A-Frame – A walkway in the shape of a cone where dogs have to walk up the incline and then come down the other side.

The Teether-Totter – Which is just like a regular one. The board will move under the dog's weight while your furry friend tries to walk across the obstacle.

To teach Buddy how to make the contact, you can start by placing treats at the ends of the obstacles. Just make sure that you start from the lowest possible position so your dog will be comfortable.

However, if Buddy is scared or refuses to go, you can try introducing them in reverse. Pick up Buddy and place him at one end so that he can take a step to take off. As he gets more comfortable, place him further and further up to make it more challenging.

Weave Poles

Weave poles are poles that Buddy will have to weave in and out of in order to succeed. This is a somewhat more challenging obstacle, so don't expect quick results and have a lot of patience.

Most trainers suggest clipping wires onto the poles to create a path that the dog can follow. First, place the poles about shoulder-width apart from Buddy and at his head's level so he cannot go under or over them. Throw a few treats onto the path to encourage him to start walking. Once he takes a step forward, praise him like crazy. As he gets comfortable, lift up the wires gradually until he can weave easily without them.

Regular Jumps

If your vet gives you the green light and says that Buddy's joints are in perfect shape, you can then introduce the jumps. However, don't start off high. If Buddy is of a small breed, place the bar on the ground. If he is of a medium breed, place the bar one inch off the ground. If he is a large dog, start with the bar only 2 inches off the ground.

To teach Buddy to jump, make sure he is leashed to avoid him having to go around the hurdle. Give specific commands for each jump, and remember to praise and reward him when he succeeds.

If Buddy is afraid to jump, practice this in a narrow hallway. Place something that blocks his way completely, and stay on the other side. Show Buddy a treat and call him to you enthusiastically. Since Buddy will have no other way but over the obstacle, eventually he will make the jump. Again, make sure not to place it too high off the ground. Praise and reward.

Tire Jumps

Start with the tire placed on the ground. Enlist a friend or a family member to hold the tire for you. Tap the tire gently to encourage your dog to go through. You can also coax him to start moving by placing some yummy treats. Let your Buddy just walk through it first. Praise and reward the good boy. Then, lift it off the ground a bit. Keep increasing the height gradually, until your dog has to jump through it. Once he does that, praise him like crazy and give him a really big treat.

Start Sequencing

Once Buddy gets comfortable with overcoming these obstacles, you can start combining them together for better results. Start by combing only two obstacles, such as the tunnels and a teeter-totter, then work your way up until Buddy has no problem in completing the whole course. When he becomes really comfortable, then you can start considering competing for real.

Conclusion

People often say that their dogs are not listening to them. But in fact, it is not so much that their furry friends don't listen, but that they don't understand what their owners are trying to tell them. I hope that this book was able to help you teach verbal cues to your dog and that you have also managed to become a bit more fluent in doggish as well.

With the information in this book, you should be able to teach Buddy basic commands as well as to take him for long walks calmly, in less than a month. Just remember, dog training is not something that you teach overnight, but a skill that should be practiced regularly in order to maintain good behavior and encourage proper discipline.

I hope that I was able to help you tame naughty Buddy, and I wish you both a long and lasting human-canine bond!

www.ingramcontent.com/pod-product-compliance
Lightning Source LLC
Chambersburg PA
CBHW060506240426
43661CB00007B/938